Advan

'Get ready to read your favourite ....ng! Honestly the first
book on the subject I've read where I didn't simultaneously experience a
rising sense of panic & think "I'm doing everything wrong!" I could hear
Mary's voice in my head as I read, each page sings with sage advice.'
Karen Koster, Ireland AM Anchor

'Mary's 'Connection not Perfection' message helps parents realize that
they are already 'good enough', and that with added knowledge and
practical tools, they can build on their connections with their children,
which are at the heart of wellbeing and resilience. Thank you Mary for
shining your light and gifting us your treasure of a book.'
Dr Malie Coyne, Clinical Psychologist and Author

'This book has all the attributes that make Dr O'Kane so popular on
Radio and TV; tremendous knowledge leavened with pragmatism and
empathy for the reality of parenting in the modern world. Mary wears
her expertise lightly and with great self-deprecation, but it comes through
in spades. Parents will put this down and feel informed, enlightened and
energised.'
Anton Savage, Broadcaster

'Dr Mary O'Kane is my kind of parenting expert - pragmatic and warm
with kindness core and centre to all her practical advice. But it's not just
kindness to children, it's kindness to ourselves as parents too as she reminds us that imperfect parenting is, actually, pretty perfect.'
Jen Hogan, Author, Journalist, Columnist.

'I will have to re-visit this book quite often for a reassuring hug on a day
when nothing seems to go quite right! Mary breaks down complex situations and simplifies them into manageable bite sized pieces. All parents
need now is a cup of coffee and this book and I can guarantee they will
feel re-energized.'
Samantha Hallows, Dublin City University.

PERFECTLY IMPERFECT PARENTING

CONNECTION NOT PERFECTION

ORLA
KELLY
PUBLISHING

Dr Mary O'Kane

Edited by Geraldine Walsh

Designed by Orla Kelly

Printed by ePrint

Cover photo by Les Germain

This book is dedicated to

Erin, Michael and Kira

My greatest teachers

CONTENTS

FOREWORD

Dr Mary O'Kane has always been a welcome and well received voice of reason and reassurance when she has appeared on my radio show. Not only for myself but for thousands of parents tuned in at home wondering and worrying if they are doing the right thing. Mary continually offers a reassuring voice whatever the issue and she has delivered this same confident, kind and practical approach to parenting in this remarkable book or the "perfect parenting guide" as I think of it.

Mary identifies so clearly how modern parenting styles have developed and how our quest for perfection is not only causing us stress as mothers and fathers, but it is not benefiting our children either. Instead she offers us reassuring and practical steps on how to encourage essential development in our children, how to achieve a connection with them and not perfection.

In this book, Mary offers complete steps to support our children of all ages to become confident and independent beings. She shows us how to build self-esteem and resilience in our children, how to support them making and maintaining friendships and how to guide them through anxiety by teaching our kids how to manage their own mental wellbeing.

We also gain from this book one of the most invaluable pieces of the puzzle - how to be patient and promote positive behaviour in our children. For me this passage in the book has changed my approach to almost everything I do with my own daughter Joan. It has grounded me again and afforded me tools to approach parenting as a better parent.

Since reading it there have been dozens of times when I stop and remind myself to let go of perfection and seek that connection with Joan. Even during times when we are both upset and emotions are heightened there are opportunities to connect with her, reassure her and support her. As mother and daughter we have had so many "perfect" days and I am thankful for that. Equally after reading this book I am now thankful that our connection has stayed intact and grown through the not so perfect days.

Being a parent is one of the most challenging roles any of us can assume in life but it is safe to say after reading (and re-reading) Perfectly Imperfect Parenting I am much better equipped for the job! Thank you, Mary.

Alison Curtis
Presenter, Weekend Breakfast Today FM

INTRODUCTION

Perfectly Imperfect Parenting:
Connection Not Perfection

The starting point for this book is simple. None of us are perfect. We need to allow ourselves the grace to accept that. Instead, a willingness to learn and develop, to connect with our children and learn and grow as they do, is at the heart of good parenting.

Growing up, my mum always told us that relationships are what really matter in life. People might think it is the money you earn, your job or social status that is important. Instead, she instilled in myself and my sisters that it is people, and our connections to them, that bring real meaning to our lives. I have always believed this, but never more so than when I had children.

For me, like most mothers, becoming a parent was a life changing experience. I remember being heavily pregnant and deciding I didn't want to give birth. I had changed my mind. I was going to stay pregnant! I was terrified of the process of birth and hadn't really thought about what lay ahead when the baby would finally come. I wasn't prepared for the absolute joy this new baby would bring. I also wasn't prepared for the absolute terror! Fear of falling down the stairs with her in my arms; fear she would slip out of my hands in the bath; fear I would damage the soft spot on her head; and as for cutting those little baby fingernails, that job was definitely reserved for my husband!

But the really big one for me was the weight of other people's expectations. While pregnant I had read various baby books which seemed to be so strict in terms of routine. Reading them made me believe I had to be perfect. This precious little lady's life was in my hands, and if I didn't get everything right, I could cause her no end of harm. Feeding and sleeping seemed to be a military operation, and for her to be happy and healthy I had to succeed at maintaining a very disciplined schedule. I learned very quickly this didn't sit well with either of us. My little lady didn't want to engage with a regimented feeding regime. She didn't want to self soothe or cry it out. Trying to achieve perfection went against everything my instincts were telling me, and the needs my baby was expressing.

What did she need from me? She needed the warmth of my skin, the softness of my touch, to sleep on my chest and breathe me in. She didn't need perfection. She needed connection.

Building Connection

Why read this book? Simply connect with them, right? That's not so difficult. Ah yes, but it's a little more complicated than that! What helps us to truly connect with them?

My learning journey in parenting has been heavily influenced by my academic work. As I studied and lectured, I realised that an understanding of psychology and child development opens a new window into how our children grow and learn. An awareness of these areas, and how we can best interact with our children based on this knowledge can change our parenting for the better. It helps us to look at *how* we connect with our children and the impact of those interactions. It helps us to appreciate our children's needs and potential, and to be more responsive to them. It was my ongoing study and research which reinforced for me the long-term value of trusting relationships and secure attachments. In this book I will describe some of the important theories from psychology and education in a simple way and explain how you can apply them to your own family.

During and after my Doctorate I examined how we can support our children as they face the challenges major transitions bring to their lives. All the evidence suggests that children who have good self-esteem and confidence, those who communicate well, are independent and can read social situations, are the children who have the smoothest transitions into adulthood. These social and emotional skills are the ones which best support our children through life. This is a reminder about what we need to invest in when it comes to parenting. The focus of this book is how we as parents can support long term social and emotional development, boost wellbeing and resilience, and help to build independence and character.

I am confident the ideas in this book will be helpful to you in your parenting. They stem from a mix of theories of past psychologists, knowledge from the field of education, and the wisdom of various advocates for children. What I have learned from all this expertise is that a background of love and affection, underpinned with scientifically proven advice, is what we need to fully support our children. The key point is that our children develop within relationships, and strong connections will result in the blossoming of their social and emotional development. Your relationship with your child is central to their development, and this book will provide simple, practical, accessible and effective guidance to support you to be the best parent you can be.

How To Use The Book

This book is not intended to be academic even though the guidance is evidence-based. It is structured with the aim of providing links between the theory and the reality of putting that theory into practice, making it accessible for parents everywhere.

I have divided the book into 8 Chapters, each addressing a different area impacting on our children's social and emotional development. As our children's development is holistic, you will find some overlap between areas. Chapter 1 begins with looking at ourselves. It is an introduction to the concept of *Good Enough Parenting* as this is the cornerstone on which the rest of the book is based. We move on to our children's development in Chapter 2. *The Confident Explorer* looks at the importance of encouraging independence, one of the most important tasks in childhood. Chapter 3, *Moving Mountains,* investigates how to support the areas of self-esteem and resilience, the foundations on which so much of our children's social and emotional development rest. Chapter 4, *Best Friends Forever*, examines the role of friendships and relationships outside the family. Chapter 5, *Parenting with Patience*, looks at how to prepare for, and respond to, our children on those challenging days. Chapter 6, *Anxious Children in an Anxious World*, looks at one of the most common mental health issues facing children and parents today. Chapter 7, *The Online Child*, considers the challenges our children face growing up in an online world. Finally, Chapter 8, *Tweens and Teens*, considers teenage wellbeing and the important transition from child to teenager to young adult. If you would like to read more on any topic discussed throughout the book, I have included a reading list of evidence.

This is not a book which requires you to start at the top of the table of contents and linearly work your way through to the end, although you might want to do that. But you can also dip in and out of it, coming back to sections you want to put into practice at different times. You will find that the thinking in each chapter is backed up by evidence. These highlighted sections are called '*The Science Bit*',

'*Learning from Psychology*' and '*What Does the Research Say?*' As I believe we can learn so much from each other, each chapter also includes insights from parents or educators on their experiences, challenges, or views related to the topic. These sections are called '*It Takes A Village*'. I would also love to be part of your village, so I have included some personal examples. You will find these in the '*From the Horse's Mouth*' sections. Finally, there are sections with advice in each chapter on how to put the theory into practice in your own life. These are called '*Top Tips!*' and '*Give it a Try!*'

I would say to any parent reading this book, have a little smile to yourself when you read parts which make perfect sense to you. These are the things you are doing already, the tools you instinctively use to improve your relationship with your child. I hope you will also find themes which add to those instincts, areas you want to develop and new ideas which you will put into practice.

Parenting can be hard sometimes. Most of us are trying our best. And our best, combined with some understanding of what is happening inside our children's brains, is good enough. This book should provide you with the knowledge and tools to support you in one of the greatest challenges of life: how to support children to have confidence and courage; to show empathy and kindness; to believe in themselves and others; and become strong and capable adults.

CHAPTER 1

THE MODERN DAY PARENT

We're all imperfect parents
And that's perfectly OK.
Tiny humans need connection,
Not perfection.
L.R. Knost

The title of this book stems from the myth that we should almost instantly become Mary Poppins when we become parents. Practically perfect in every way. Instead, wouldn't it be better to aim to be the parent which L.R. Knost describes in such a beautiful and empathetic way? To be the parent who values connection with their children, instead of worrying about being perfect.

The aim of this book is to look at how we as parents can support our children's social and emotional development, building their well-being and resilience, independence and character. But before we look at how we can go about this, let's take a look at ourselves, and the role of parents in society today.

Good Enough Parenting

Parenting today can be very demanding. In my parents and grandparents' generations, children were allowed to fend for themselves to a much greater extent. There was not the same emphasis on being the perfect parent which we are exposed to today. From the moment we find out we are pregnant, or oftentimes before that if a couple are trying to become pregnant, we are surrounded with advice on how we should behave. Everyone appreciates a little guidance at times, but the level of judgement that goes along with this advice is huge. We have set the bar, in terms of perfect parenting, remarkably high. The pressure on parents to conform to a very idealised standard is continuous.

Let's remember we are allowed to make mistakes, and to learn every day throughout our parenting lives. Battling perfectionism amid a tirade of emotions, questions, personalities, and a whole lot of growing up, is not the way to go. Being good enough is pretty much where the winning in parenting lies.

 Learning from Psychology

The concept of *good enough mothering* was developed by Donald Winnicott in his book *Playing and Reality*[1]. As there were primarily mothers looking after children at that time, his work refers to mothers alone, however, his ideas are equally appropriate for fathers and indeed all primary carers. Good enough is an important idea to consider.

Winnicott starts by reminding us that babies are psychologically fragile, so their caregivers should be highly attuned to their needs in the first few months of life. But he argues we should naturally move from an initial feeling of devotion to the child to an understanding that we cannot meet their every need.

This is important as the child needs to experience minor frustrations within their world. He believed this was of benefit to their development, and reasoned that children need to experience small disappointments in order to better equip themselves to face life's challenges. As the child experiences these minor blips they learn to tolerate some frustration.

He argues that none of us could sustain being perfect long term. We cannot give our child our undivided attention 24 hours a day, every day. His point is that this benefits our children as they need us to occasionally let them down so they can learn to survive and thrive in an imperfect world. They are learning in small ways that the world doesn't revolve around them!

Winnicott's aim was to remove pressure from mothers, however, one criticism of his work was his emphasis on the mother alone. The expectation was that the mother should shoulder the full responsibility for the child, and that she was responsible for how that child develops. We now use the term, *good enough parent*, in recognition that the role of parent, or primary caregiver, does not always reside with the mother.

So when you are feeling guilty that you were not able to respond to your child's needs immediately; when you are feeling guilty that they were crying in their car seat and you had to continue your journey; when you were feeling guilty that you could not be in two places at once, remind yourself that you are preparing them to deal with the minor disappointments in life. They are learning that these frustrations happen to all children, and importantly, they can survive them.

Parenting is not about perfection, it is about being there for your child, and connecting with them.

The Impact of our Beliefs

I don't like to use the terms Helicopter or Lawnmower Parenting, but the principles behind them are something we need to consider when we think about empowering our children. No-one wants to be a Helicopter Parent, hovering over their child in the playground in case they fall, mediating minor issues with friends, and taking on every task for their children. Nor do they want to be a Lawnmower Parent forging ahead removing any obstacle the child may face. Neither approach does our children any favours. We clear a little path for them because we don't want them to struggle, when in fact, it is supporting independence which allows the child to grow stronger. And yet, our approach to parenting today encourages us to be ever present, to engage in the 'work' of parenting as we would a competitive sport. Why do we seek perfection in this role?

The concept of good enough parenting does not sit easily with everyone. Many of us consider our role as parents to be the most high-stakes job of our lives. Indeed, many of us have invested a lot into this role. We may have made professional sacrifices, financial sacrifices, and personal sacrifices in the name of parenthood. The concept of good enough parenting feels like lowering the bar, lowering our expectations, lowering our standards. But the important point to remember is that to be the best parent we can be means being human. While we should be caring and empathetic, we do not have to be faultless. As Winnicott says, our flaws are necessary for independent development to take place. Is it possible that this picture-perfect parenting style, where we put so much pressure on ourselves, does not produce the results we are aiming for?

What Does the Research Say?

Research from San Diego State University[2] examined changes in the behaviour of teenagers in America over the past five decades. It found huge differences in our teens and their earlier counterparts. Two specific findings from this study really stood out for me.

The first was the rapid decline of individual sense of control. Our teens were much less likely to believe they were in control of their own lives than teens decades ago. This is important as this sense of personal control is linked to greater success in life, and lower levels of mental health issues. The average teen in 2002 felt less control over their destiny than 80% of teens in the 1960s did! Another change noted in the research was a change from intrinsic to extrinsic goals during the same period. This means as compared to students in the 60s and 70s, our teens have moved from being motivated by goals involving personal development, health, and relationships with others, to more external areas such as material gain, status, and validation from others.

The findings suggest that our teens today feel they have little control over their lives and are also very reliant on external sources of validation. This is a worrying combination.

Could these changes be linked to how we parent today? Professor Peter Gray from Boston University has studied this area for many years and argues that this is the case[3]. He believes that a reduced sense of control, difficulties with emotional regulation, and increased levels of social isolation for our children, are linked to how society sees parenting today. His argument is that we over-protect our children and tend to deprive them of free play without adult control. By doing this, we are depriving them of the learning opportunities which develop important skills. In our effort to protect them we, in fact, hinder them.

From the Horse's Mouth

When I was a child my family had a caravan in Arklow where we, along with all our cousins, would head every summer. As children we would head out the door each morning and the caravan park was ours to roam. Off we went, only to come back when we were hungry. We laughed, we cried, we fought, we played, and mostly we looked out for each other. What did we learn over those summers? We learned problem solving and decision-making skills; we learned conflict resolution and how to bargain and negotiate; we learned social skills, and lessons in friendship. We learned that we were strong and capable, and that when things went wrong, we could pick ourselves back up and handle the challenges we faced. We learned a lot of these lessons because our parents gave us the freedom to grow and explore. They didn't think they had to be the perfect parents monitoring our progress. The demands they placed on us, and on themselves, were possibly more realistic that those expected of parents today. So why did this change?

My parents and grandparents' generations let their children run out the door every day believing they were safe. They thought the world was a safe place and their children would come to no harm. But later in life they found out that their children had in fact come to harm. So, my generation, and the parents after us, became scared. We were so frightened by the experiences of past generations that we turned full circle and became fearful to let our children out of our sight. We became the playdate generation. We had coffee in each other's houses while dutifully keeping an eye on our children.

If we heard a piercing cry from the garden, we all jumped up, and ran to investigate [secretly hoping that ours was the child who had been injured, and not the one who had done the injuring, as that would reflect on our parenting!] We have become so scared that something might happen to our children that we have created the perfect storm. We drive them everywhere, we overschedule their lives, we warn them about all the perceived dangers in the world. Most of our teens have grown up getting a very consistent message from us that the world is a dangerous place. We do everything we can to protect them from harm, but at what cost?

I want to make clear this is not about blaming parents. It is a natural instinct to want to protect our children. Indeed, one of our jobs as a parent is to shelter, care for and guide them.

Trying to be the perfect parent is exhausting. We are on alert constantly trying to pre-empt every possible difficulty. We reassure ourselves that because we are doing everything right, nothing bad will ever happen to our children. But that is not the case. It is possible that in our quest for perfection, in our mission to become super-parents, we have forgotten that being perfect is not something that comes easily to most of us. In fact, imperfection is part of the human condition.

Taking on board the above research in combination with Winnicott's views on being good enough, we know there is no need to strive for perfection. Let's remember that good enough parents know they will make mistakes but still strive to do their best. Good enough parents know their children will make mistakes, but that this is part of the learning process. Good enough parents try to understand the needs of their children and understand their perspectives. Good enough parents know that the core of what we do is to create a strong and lasting connection that will carry us through the tough times.

The Village of Parenthood

We should also allow each other the same grace. We each make our own choices about our parenting decisions, and what works best for us as individual families. Being good enough recognises that the choices and circumstances of other parents might differ.

 From the Horse's Mouth

Over the past five years or so I have found great support as a mother from the community of parents who follow my Facebook page. They remind me on a daily basis that as parents, and for me as a mother, we go through the same struggles.

So let me say, well done to the mothers who have natural births, home births, water births, drug assisted births, caesareans, adopt or foster their children. Each one loves their child and wants to do the best for them. Well done to the mothers who love to breast feed, and to those who struggle with breast feeding but persevere as they want to have that connection with their baby. Well done to the mothers who bottle feed, some by choice, some by necessity. Well done to the mothers who stay at home to be with their children, well done to the working mums who balance home and family life, and well done to those with part-time jobs being pulled in all directions.

The concept of being "raised by a village" is one we might consider harking back to. Instead of criticising each other, we can try to support the choices of other parents, even if they are not our own.

Our Inner Critical Voices

When we are not facing the criticisms of others, we are often self-critical about our own parenting skills. From when our two-year-old throws a tantrum in the middle of the supermarket, to the primary school child who cannot get their spellings right when the rest of the class are getting gold stars. When our tween refuses to read any books while her friends seem to devour them, to our teen-ager who hates to take part in sports while their cousin is captain of the A team. We tend to judge our children, and ourselves, by the weight of other people's expectations.

 It Takes a Village

Imposter syndrome is a challenge. We often see other mums lives as the blockbuster and ours as the bloopers reel. The reality is that we all experience little bits of both every day. Maybe give ourselves a little more credit for the magic moments and a little more tolerance when it all feels a little chaotic.

[Credit: Fiona Scott via Facebook]

From the moment we start making comparisons between our children and their peers, those critical voices inside our heads often judge our children, and our own parenting. And very harshly too. When we worry about what others think, our parenting judgement becomes thwarted. We make decisions which are not necessarily suitable to our family and their needs. As parents, the need to compete with other parents or to constantly compare our children to others, does us no good. It can be hard to avoid comparison, we all do it at times, but it is unfair to ourselves and our children.

Instead, we need to remind ourselves that every child develops at their own pace. Rather than compare our children to others, comparing them to their younger selves is much more beneficial. In this way we can see how they are growing and developing. Different children have different strengths and different ways of making sense of the world. By observing them as individuals, we can see their individual achievements and progress. This can also help us to identify where they might need some support. Childhood is not a race. Each child should be given the time and support they need to flourish at their own pace.

Let's not forget to do the same when we are considering our own parenting. Instead of making comparisons to friends and family, look at how our own understanding of our children, their strengths, and any needs they might have, are developing. Many of us over analyse our parenting decisions, worrying whether we have made the right choices, agonising over past decisions. Recognising we cannot control everything is a big lesson. Every family has its own challenges, and we all struggle in different ways. We all have different lives, and different views on parenting. Remind yourself that every parent makes mistakes in their parenting, but hopefully we learn from them. Forgive yourself for past errors, and instead focus on continuing to develop as a parent, along with your child's natural development.

It is worth remembering, even though no two children are the same and no two parents are the same, our goals are quite similar. We may have a different approach to parenting, but we have one important thing in common. We all want the best for our children. We want them to be kind and compassionate. We want them to be confident and have good self-esteem. We want them to make friends and thrive socially and emotionally. We want them to grow to be independent as they make their own way in the world. We want them to believe they can achieve whatever they set their minds to. This is not the Olympics. Parenting is not a competitive sport. It is about supporting the needs of our children and guiding them so they can hopefully reach for their own dreams.

With all of this in mind, let's move onto considering the social and emotional skills we want to support in our children. The skills which will prepare them for life.

CHAPTER 2

THE CONFIDENT EXPLORER –
INDEPENDENCE SKILLS

Prepare your child for the path, not the path for your child.
Tim Elmore

Developing independence is one of the most important jobs of childhood. We want our children to grow to have the skills to function well in society with minimal support. Of course, we want them to know we are available for support and guidance, but as our children grow, they should become more independent in the basic areas of their lives. This gradual process of separation prepares our children for the demands of adulthood and is something they have been preparing for since birth.

The Infant Brain

From birth to about age five, our children's brains grow at an incredible rate, doubling in size during the first year. At birth babies have all the brain cells they will need in adult life however it is the connections between these which continue to develop. For babies we know that at least a million new neural connections are made every second, and up to 80% of brain connections are formed within the first three years. Our child's experiences during this time help shape how their brain develops. Their connection to us plays a crucial role in how their brains are built.

 The Science Bit!

The areas of the brain which are responsible for different tasks develop at different rates. Sensory pathways develop first, followed by language skills and higher-level thinking skills. The various functions of the brain work in a very coordinated way suggesting that emotional wellbeing, social development, and cognitive skills are all interlinked. The early years are the most important years for developing these connections as the brain is most flexible, or 'plastic' during this period.

As we get older the brain becomes more specialised, meaning it becomes more difficult for it to reorganise and adapt. If the connections needed for some of the higher-level skills are not formed during the early years, it can be more difficult for them to be made later in life. It is our early experiences and interactions which influence brain development, making this an important reminder of how relationships are hugely important for brain development.

We know that babies come into the world pre-programmed for interaction. They are immediately equipped to make connections with others. This makes sense from an evolutionary perspective as they are completely dependent on others to respond to their basic needs. And yet, many historical studies tell us that babies need more than their physical needs met in order to thrive. Their brains are designed to relate to human features such as faces and voices, and to seek out interactions. They come into the world ready to make connections.

 Learning from Psychology

Children are not the only ones pre-programmed in this way. Studies with young monkeys conducted by Harry Harlow[4] (1958) also explored this issue. Harlow found that young monkeys who were given a choice between two 'mother surrogate' models would choose a mother who had a soft cloth towelling surface rather than a mother made from wire mesh which had an attached milk bottle for feeding. This happened even though the cloth mother did not deliver any food. When these infant monkeys were put into a new room the presence of the cloth mother calmed them. The monkey was used as what Harlow called a *base for operations* from which they would explore, while periodically returning to the mother surrogate. The bond with the soft object was more important than the provision of food.

Babies also seem predisposed to engage in what we call *meshing behaviours*. This is when the adult and child's behaviours fit in with each other during social interactions. Research where mothers are asked to stop communicating with their babies during interactions, show us how babies respond with distress to a lack of response from the mother. We also know that mothers instinctively progressively allow their babies to take a more active role in these interactions. Therefore, the interaction slowly becomes a turn-taking interaction between the pair. We see this often when a parent communicates with their baby using *parentese*, a simple sing-song type of speech reserved for babies. The mother repeats, "ma-ma…ma-ma" while gazing at her baby and using animated facial gestures. The baby responds back to mum by cooing and smiling. This is turn provokes another enthusiastic response from the mother, "Yes baby girl! ma-ma...ma-ma." Baby responds by gurgling and reaching out towards her mother, and the dance continues!

Secure Attachments

We know the early years are vitally important and that, from birth, babies connect with those around them. But how do these interactions impact on their development?

Warm loving relationships provide comfort and are the way in which babies develop a sense of their own worth. As caregivers respond to the cries, facial expressions and gestures of infants, the first lines of communication are opened. When the baby realises their needs will be met, it helps them to develop trust. It is no surprise that when speaking about infants we stress the importance of these secure relationships.

The concept of secure attachment was developed by British psychologist John Bowlby who referred to attachments as being all important for the healthy mental development of young children[5]. He suggested that infants and young children need to experience warm, continuous, and mutually responsive relationships with those closest to them. If a child is frightened, she will seek out her primary caregiver, seeking comfort and care. This makes sense in terms of survival as children who maintain proximity to their primary carer are more likely to survive into adulthood. This relationship teaches children they can depend on their needs to be consistently met, which is the foundation for secure attachment.

The child develops an internal working model (a personal theory) of how the world works based on these interactions. As this relationship provides the support the child needs, they will seek it out at times of fear. They use it as a secure base from which they can explore the world. Bowlby's work led to the argument that children who grow up to demonstrate independence and self-reliance have parents who are supportive when needed, but who also encourage independence and autonomy.

It seems that the parent intuitively provides a holding relationship for the infant. They use empathy to provide a reliable environment, responsive to the needs of the child. We often see parents do this by engaging in mirroring the responses of the baby, responding to the baby's expressions, and reflecting their love back in their responses. These exchanges between the parent and child enable the baby to build a sense of themselves.

If we consider the example of a baby dropping things from her highchair only to have the parent pick them up and return them, we can see how the baby gradually learns to take a risk and let something go, safe in the knowledge that it will return. The baby also learns they can gradually move away from the parent and tolerate the parents' absence. Basically, these first attachments when the baby is very dependent on the parent are a contributing factor towards their independence.

Connection is what gives us the self-belief to then take flight!

This does not have to be a perfect partnership, but there must be a good enough fit between both partners – parent and child – to support the child through the process of development and growth. This message of good enough is one we all need to hear repeatedly until it becomes firmly established in our minds. It is something we will come back to again and again throughout this book.

One of the most important goals of a parent in this relationship is to raise children who become independent and self-reliant. The ability to do things for yourself, including decision making and taking responsibility for your actions, is important for our children's confidence and resilience. We want them to grow to have the skills to function well in society with minimal support. To do this, they need to learn to gradually take on responsibility for themselves. However, encouraging them to do this is something many of us struggle with – and I most definitely include myself in this!

 From the Horse's Mouth

We are under immense pressure these days, not only from the burden of trying to be perfect parents but also from incredible time pressures. So much so, we tend to do too much for our children. I remember when my children were younger, my eldest was in Second Cass, my son in Junior Infants, and my baby was usually on my hip. I always seemed to be rushing in the mornings and depended on my eldest daughter to be independent while I ran around trying to get us all out the door for the school run. My son would come down the stairs and sit like a little prince on the bottom of the stairs, with his shoes perched beside him. With the baby on my hip, I would grab his foot, open the Velcro shoe, pop his foot inside, close the Velcro, and repeat! In case he wasn't pampered enough, sometimes I would then zip up his coat for him and there he was ready to go! Oh, dear!

One day I stopped to think about what I was doing and the unintentional messages I was giving him. Not only was I showing him that I didn't think he could do the job as well as I could, but I was also telling him that I trusted his elder sister to do the job herself. Although it was the last thing I intended, I was either giving him the message that he was a little prince, there to be pampered, or that he was incapable of looking after himself!

When I stood back to look at my morning routine, I realised I was so stressed and rushed that I was not allowing him to be independent even though he was very capable. I know at other times in my children's lives I have had to stop myself doing the same thing; taking over their responsibilities because I thought I could do the task faster, or better. It is something I became aware of as they grew up, and I don't think I am alone in this.

As parents many of us need to remind ourselves just how capable our children are, and to encourage them to be as independent as they are developmentally ready for.

Scaffolding Our Children

When we give our children independence, they learn to feel competent. They need to be exposed to challenges to know they can manage and cope. A bit like a vaccination acts as a trial run for the immune system.

We noted earlier that when our children are born, they are completely dependent on us as parents to take care of them. We are genetically predisposed to respond to their cries. As children grow it is important to gradually remove the supports and allow them to become more independent. One way we can do this is to scaffold our children's learning. Psychologists have long argued that acting in this way is all important to their independence. Just as scaffolding is used on a building to support it during construction, our support needs to be withdrawn as our child grows more independent. Our role as parents and educators is to assist them only when needed. As they progress and become more independent, we adjust the level of support needed to encourage our children's confidence. In this way, we can help them achieve tasks they would not be able to achieve alone, building their independence as we go.

Learning from Psychology

Within the area of Education the concept of scaffolding children's learning is an important part of the classroom. The term is linked to the work of Russian Psychologist Lev Vygotsky and his theory on children's cognitive development. He proposes that children are active learners and develop through social interaction with others, particularly those who are more knowledgeable than they are. Practitioners will look for the *Zone of Proximal Development* which is the space in which the child can almost perform a task independently but needs a little assistance, or scaffolding. The practitioner changes the level of support provided to the child as they progress independently. Questions are often used to promote learning – "I wonder what would happen if…?" The level of guidance is adjusted according to the level of the child's performance. This adult guidance enables the child to achieve a skill they would not have been able to attain alone.

This approach sees the child as actively constructing their own learning through collaboration with their teachers or more experienced peers. Parents can also foster learning by delivering

> opportunities which provide these challenges for the child, while using guided instruction to support their development. This concept can help us as parents to think about what our children can achieve at the present, and very gently push them out of their comfort zones with minimum support to achieve greater things.

Learning from Mistakes

When our little ones are learning to walk, we see them tentatively take those first steps, and we are aware of the bravery it takes to let go of the sofa and give walking a try! They take those first steps and revel in the excitement it causes for everyone watching. What usually happens after a few steps? Yes, whoosh, down they come onto their bottom! Neither the baby or the excited onlookers view this as a mistake, instead we smile and laugh. In my house, it would get an "Oopsie Daisy" and we encourage them to get back on their feet and try again. These little ones are so brave. On they go. They keep trying and see every attempt as something to be proud of. But what happens as they grow older? Many of us seem to lose that optimistic approach to life and its challenges.

Mistakes are an important part of learning, but many children see these lapses as painful. In order to cope with difficulties in adulthood we need to encourage them to face their own challenges, scaffolding them if necessary, as mentioned above. As much as we would like to smooth every path for them, it is in their best interests to become independent and take responsibility for their own lives.

We would love our children to live in sun filled days, with never a cloud in the sky. But life isn't like that. The rainy days will come. Instead of teaching them to wait for sunny weather, we need to prepare them to face into the wind, knowing that they can survive the storm.

By trying to avoid our children struggling in any way, we are creating a generation who cannot cope with adversity. Although we have the best of intentions when we try to solve all their problems this results in children and teens who struggle with challenges and cannot cope with the idea of mistakes or failure. Learning from their mistakes is a valuable skill enabling our children to take responsibility for their actions.

This learning is a key skill in developing independence and resilience. Encouraging lots of opportunities for them to practice these new skills may mean having the patience ourselves to allow them to fail, learn from their mistakes, and try again. Yes, this might take additional time and planning, but when we consider the long-term gains, it is worth it.

Watching our children fail elicits an emotional response from most parents. We want to step in, protect them, rescue them, make it better. We feel their pain and will do anything we can to prevent it. One way to avoid this happening, is to start small. Rather than letting them jump in and experience failure in a high-stakes situation, step back and give them autonomy over little things. Let them experience mistakes in small everyday ways, where they can learn from failure, with an opportunity to try again. Be present for feedback or guidance, but not to direct proceedings.

We also tend to judge our own parenting on their success. So, we feel for our children, but our own self-worth as a parent can be dented when we see them struggle. If we view our children's success as an indicator of our own performance, we are tempted to become more directive, and take control. We let our anxiety about our own success as parents override our aim to strengthen their coping skills. Instead we can stop equating doing everything for our children as being a perfect parent. Remind ourselves that our children are not perfect, and neither are we, but all of us are doing our best, and learning as we go.

👍 Give it a Try!

Persistence amid frustration is a valuable skill for our children to develop and will stand to them in becoming more independent. How can we support our children to become more persistent?

- Encourage children to see mistakes as learning experiences. By trying again, children learn that obstacles can be overcome.

- Once they reach a goal, remember to praise not only the end result, but also their willingness to stick with the task.

- Aim to give children lots of opportunities to practice and master their skills, letting them overcome the fear of failure, but supporting them so they keep trying.

- When things go wrong, talk with them about what they learned. What would they do differently next time? Remember, particularly with a teenager, to let a little time pass before helpfully asking them what they might have done differently! Allow them time to process the perceived failure before getting them to consider what they might learn from it.

- A great way to encourage persistence is to allow them to discreetly overhear you praising their effort and perseverance to someone else. They may not believe us if we remind them how we are proud of them after a defeat, but they often believe us if they hear us telling someone else – she told Granny, so it must be true!

- We can also model persistence by telling our child about situations when we made a mistake, and how difficult that was. Then tell them what we learned from it, and how we would now approach the situation.

- Finally, we can support them by letting them know we love them even when they fail or make bad decisions.

I am an absolute believer in giving our children a chance if they mess up at something. But, if they continue to make the same mistakes over again, they need to learn to face the consequences. For instance, if they keep forgetting their PE kit, they may need to learn they cannot take part in the activity. If they haven't done their homework, allow them to explain why to the teacher themselves. If they break their retainer, let them explain what happened to the dentist. Make them take responsibility for their actions. It is not about abandoning them. If they have worked hard on a school project and in a genuine mistake, they leave it on the kitchen table, I would bring it to them. But if they keep forgetting their lunch and expect you to bring it to school, don't! The ability to deal with the consequences of their actions will stand to them.

In doing all of this, it is important we encourage our children to approach difficult situations as opportunities for growth. The world isn't perfect, we cannot just make our children happy. Instead we should look for opportunities for them to grow as individuals and become more resilient. Reminding ourselves of our children's strengths and capabilities will instil our confidence in them to make independent decisions.

 It Takes a Village

Fill their cup, help kids know their strengths, give them activities that will build their belief in themselves, and always point out how they have overcome things when they weren't quite sure they could. I always remind my son how brave, courageous, and determined he is. He's even telling us now, don't give up, be patient. It becomes part of their automatic thinking when they are faced with challenges and teaches them coping strategies.

[Credit: Jane Foden via Facebook]

Taking on Household Chores

One of the ways in which we can help give our children the confidence to take responsibility for themselves is to give them jobs to do around the house. This also helps to develop independence.

We often say children should be able to relax and enjoy their childhood as the years pass so quickly. We also know children today can be very overscheduled and often have little free time. But doing jobs around the house supports so many different skill sets, from self-reliance to competence. It's good for them to learn about cleaning and cooking. Being tidy and clean is probably not a priority for most children - we need to help them to see the value of these things!

Taking on jobs in the house also teaches them that each member of the family should play a role in maintaining the household, and that it's not all me, me, me! They realise that life involves work, and how it is important that we all contribute our share to the family and home. Remember, they don't have to be sent off to take on these tasks alone, we can work together to get jobs done.

 What Does the Research Say?

Research supports giving our children household chores. The Harvard Grant Study[6], the longest running longitudinal study in history, followed university students in the U.S. for over 75 years, and found those who did chores as children gained important life skills which enabled them to do better in later life. Taking on household tasks helped the teens develop a stronger work ethic which lasted throughout their lives. In fact, the researchers felt that doing these household jobs in childhood was the best predictor of the child becoming a happy, healthy, and independent adult!

These tasks made children feel more competent, gave them a sense of accomplishment, and encouraged them to become good citizens. The younger the child who took on these tasks, the stronger the impact. The researchers suggest that the reason for this is not only becoming aware of themselves as independent and competent, but also they become adults who see a task that needs to be completed and take responsibility for doing it.

In practice many of us no longer give our children jobs to do around the house. A recent Braun Research poll in the US found 28% percent of parents gave chores, although 82% percent had to do chores themselves as children. There are a few reasons for this finding. Our busy lives could be one of the main reasons. Sometimes it feels like too much effort to support them in taking on a task. If we do the job ourselves, we know it will get done the way we want it, and we won't have to deal with arguments or delays. But as with the example of my son as a child, think about the message this sends our children. When we over-help them we show no faith in them. They need to see what they can achieve themselves.

Parents often ask what specific jobs children should be taking on at different ages. All children are different, they grow and develop at different rates, but here are some ideas for age-appropriate jobs which children might take on at various ages.

Chores for Little Ones

Little ones can start with jobs like picking up their toys, helping to clean up after a friend has been over to play, and fixing the duvet back on their bed every morning. Remember to be very specific when asking them to complete a task. Asking a pre-schooler to clean up the playroom can feel overwhelming for them. But asking them to pick up the Lego off the floor and put it in the Lego box is more specific and more realistic.

They are usually happier taking on a task with a little company even if you, or an older sibling are tidying up something else in the same room.

Usually our children, particularly the little ones, can enjoy doing real jobs, in fact that is the basis of the Montessori method of education. Allow your little ones take on real household tasks now. Don't wait until you feel they are capable. By the time they're older and more competent they may well have lost interest! For example, young children will often love something like mopping the floor. They might not do a fantastic job, but if they are keen, encourage it. You are teaching them that being part of a family means playing their part. They are part of a team and helping around the house encourages teamwork.

Learning from Psychology:

Maria Montessori (1870-1952) was an Italian educator who founded the Montessori method of education. Her goal, to allow for children's intellectual, physical, emotional and social development, was very different to most education systems at the time. Montessori saw the role of the adult as a guide, present to stimulate the child, but acting as an observer allowing the child to think for themselves. Central to her method is the triad of the child, the teacher and the environment. Her method of education is characterised by providing a *prepared environment* which offers children opportunities to work with interesting and freely chosen work. The aim is to learn by engaging hands-on with the materials in activities which support long periods of concentration. The first Montessori materials that a child usually encounters are those from the practical life curriculum. These are activities that are familiar to the child, such as pouring different materials, cleaning and polishing, setting a table, doing and undoing clothing fasteners. The tasks all aim to take care of the person, of others, and the environment. By completing these tasks children develop control of movement and coordination. But they also develop the child's skills for independent living.

Chores for Primary School Age

At primary school age children can start to take more responsibility both in the house and for school related items. They can have responsibility for things like putting away their school bags, putting gym gear in the wash basket, and making lunches. As they get older, tasks like planning to have their football kit clean for the Saturday game are important for them to learn.

Again, remember to be specific when asking them to complete tasks. We might ask our child to clean their bedroom and be surprised when we come back an hour later and they are sitting on the bed playing with an old game they have rediscovered. But perhaps they had put away their toys, ignoring the clothes lying on their bed or floor, and in their eyes this was in effect cleaning their room. Make very clear, step by step, what you expect them to do for each task. Always praise the effort they put into the task, but don't expect perfection! Be specific when praising their work. The best feedback is honest and accurate.

Chores for Tweens and Teens

Our tweens and teens can again take on even more responsibility. Paying them pocket money for chores can be a great way of teaching them financial responsibility, but jobs like keeping their room clean are often expected as part of family life rather than a job that earns them cash. Some parents like to use a token system in place of pocket money where the child earns tokens towards an activity or an outing they like, or even screen time. One of the important aspects of taking on jobs around the house as our children get older is that they are learning jobs which will be important for them in the real world. Make sure they are learning cooking skills, how to do their laundry, and life skills which they will need in the future.

👍 **Give it a Try!**

Some Age Appropriate Household Chores

Ages 2-3	Ages 4-6
Make bed (fix duvet!)	Set the table
Help feed pets	Match socks from laundry
Put toys away	Help make school lunches
Help set the table	Help with food preparation
Watering flowers / garden plants	Clear table after dinner
Help when you are changing baby	Wipe down kitchen table
Clear silverware from dishwasher	Sweep the kitchen floor
Ages 7-9	**Ages 10-12**
Put groceries away	Walk the dog
Make easy snacks	Make a simple meal
Simple baking	Clean kitchen after dinner
Folding laundry	Hoover floors
Put away clean clothes	Mop the floors
Wipe down kitchen counters	Sort recycling
Loading dishwasher	General gardening chores
Emptying dishwasher	Help with small DIY tasks

Age 13+	
Mow the lawn	Clean bathroom
Clean the car inside and out	Take sheets off bed
Iron clothes	Shop for some groceries
Watch younger siblings	Cook a full lunch / dinner

The idea of taking on these tasks is that they are making a progression towards becoming more independent. It is a laddering approach. They are slowly climbing the steps on a ladder, progressing towards more complex and demanding tasks. Allow them to try, fail, and try again until they get it right. Instead of giving them fish, we are teaching them to fish for themselves!

 Top Tip!

It can work well to encourage them to take on tasks they enjoy, or at least avoid the ones they hate! We might think forcing them to take on a task they hate is toughening them up for life's tough jobs, but it could have the opposite effect and put them off completely.

True independence also involves the desire to complete the task. Rather than doing the task to secure adult approval, you want them to see the value and sense of achievement in completing the task. If you engage them in tasks they enjoy, they are more likely to be intrinsically motivated to continue.

Independence and Risk

As well as household tasks you may also consider the age at which you want them to be able to take on more independence in their everyday lives. Try not to base these decisions on what other children in their class are doing, although most of our children will try to use this as an argument! Instead, these decisions are personal for each family, based on the age and maturity of their child. Some of the questions to consider will also be based on where you live, and your individual circumstances. For example, at what age are they able to walk to school on their own? At what age can they run to the local shop on a quick errand? At what age can they stay home alone? At what age can they mind a younger sibling?

 What Does the Research Say?

A 2018 survey in the UK of 2,000 parents by 'MyNametags' found a general consensus that children should be able to:

- Age 7: ride a bike
- Age 8: put their own clothes in the wash
- Age 9: have pocket money
- Age 10: have friends over for sleepovers
- Age 11: have a TV in their bedroom
- Age 12: walk or cycle to school on their own
- Age 13: be alone in the house
- Age 14: be trusted with a key to the door
- Age 15: go on a date
- Age 16: go out with friends after dark

Would you agree with the ages for this list of milestones?

One issue we need to consider when looking at our attitude to encouraging independence, and giving children more freedom in their everyday lives, is our own attitude to risk. Deciding on the right amount of responsibility and independence is a balancing act for most parents. Over the years, we have become so concerned with protecting our children, that we often deprive them of opportunities for independence. We have become so risk adverse, that we let unfounded fears prevent us from allowing our children the freedom they need to grow.

Developmentally, children are designed to teach themselves emotional resilience through engaging in risky play - climbing trees, wrestling, chasing and so on. Risky play, very often outdoors, can be important in supporting independence.

The Science Bit!

Young mammals of most species engage in similar play; play fighting, climbing heights, running at speed, and hiding from each other. We know that there is an evolutionary value to these types of risky play. Interestingly, young children and animals also enjoy taking the most vulnerable role in these games. Evolutionary childhood research tells us that it is through this type of play that children learn to judge risk and develop the cognitive skills to make more accurate judgements about levels of risk and safety. It seems that exposure to risk strengthens the ability to realistically manage risky situations. Playing in this way allows the child to work out how the world works, and how their bodies work, in the context of a safe space.

Particularly in western cultures there has been a decline in opportunities for free play without adult control. Anxiety has increased dramatically during this period, and there may well be a connection. Freedom to take age-appropriate risks helps children to learn emotional regulation and decision-making skills. It teaches them they can cope when things go wrong, that they can manage their fear and overcome it. As an adult, our role involves knowing when to step back, and allow our children the freedom and independence to test their limits and problem solve themselves.

Over-protectiveness on our part impacts on their ability to reach their own goals. Children who are not allowed independence, go on to believe they are not capable of independence, so it becomes a self-fulfilling prophesy. Instead, if we as parents allow our children to take on tasks they feel ready and capable of, but have not yet been allowed to do, we are empowering the child. This could be to walk their dog alone, walk to school with friends, any activity they consider challenging but feel ready to take on. We want to encourage safe risk-taking, giving children opportunities to be more independent, and allowing them to grow and develop.

Another way of doing this is to allow children greater freedom to negotiate their own differences and play freely without adult interference. Leaving our children and their friends to their own devices to develop their own games encourages greater imagination. Allowing them to play in mixed age groups is also reported to increase confidence in children, encouraging a shift in maturity. One way to do the above is through outdoor activity.

Engaging with Nature

A lack of outdoor experiences can lead children to become less competent both physically and mentally. We know the rise in obesity, attention-deficit disorder, and depression have been linked to the growing decline in children's outdoor play.

The term *nature-deficit disorder* has been used to describe how modern children rarely spend time alone exploring nature.

The area in which parents allow their children to stray from their supervision has shrunk rapidly in the past few decades. This is due in part to our contemporary culture of fear, and in part to a rise in anxiety about personal injury. It appears that the health and safety culture is impacting on everyday children's activities such as climbing trees and running in the playground. Research suggests that the way our children spend their time has dramatically changed in recent decades. This pattern started in the 1940's when the time children spent in free play within their local neighbourhood started to reduce and has been consistently declining since that point. But a lack of free play results in a reduction in learning opportunities. Children are naturally drawn to risky play, and by engaging in what we call safe risk-taking outdoors in nature, they develop both physically and mentally in different ways than when they are shut off from the natural world.

Instead of a focus in keeping children *as safe as possible* it may help if we reframe this as keeping them *as safe as necessary*.

Taking this safe as necessary approach can help to support children to grow in confidence, self-esteem, resilience, and reach their full potential. We can encourage independence and resilience by allowing our children to experience and overcome challenges with a sense of adventure rather than fear.

Over recent years, we are all becoming more aware of the importance of a connection with the outdoors through hands-on experiences in a positive risk-benefit environment. Have a look at the case study below which highlights how children learn and develop while engaging with the outdoors. We can see how the issue is resolved by child-initiated thinking, with the adults on hand to offer support only if needed.

 It Takes a Village

The Story of The Missing Trowel:

'Later in the term, on a dry day when the hole was still full of water from an overnight downpour, I noticed a lot of activity around the deep puddle. Four or five 3-4-year olds were in a deep discussion and were clearly trying to solve a problem. As I watched, they appeared to be trying to extract something from the depth of the puddle. It was too deep to reach by hand. One child employed a stick to try to remove the object, but to no avail. I watched as a third collected a colander and tried to remove water from the puddle, whilst another child used a bucket to add water to the puddle (apparently in an attempt to float the object out). Tempted as I was to 'wade in' and offer my own suggestions, I waited and watched. Another child joined in and said he was bigger and could reach into the puddle. Standing astride it, he reached into the puddle and found that he too did not have long enough arms to retrieve the object. Finally, the child who had originally used the colander (having realised that it was an ineffective tool for her purpose) returned with a bucket and began to remove water efficiently. Eventually the water was shallow enough for 3-year-old Amy to reach into the puddle and grasp the trowel with her hand. She raised it into the air and announced triumphantly 'I've got it'! What a collaborative and sustained effort for those children!'

[Menna Godfrey[7], Educator, Open University, E110 Module]

This example highlights the value in allowing children to engage in a risk-benefit environment when their thinking was challenged. Children learn best from active engagement with the environment. Engaging with nature in the outdoors offers children opportunities to become more independent learners, developing confidence in themselves and their ability to control their world.

Remember you don't need a forest or woodland on your door-step to get your child outside. For young children there are so many ways in which they can be encouraged to actively engage with the outdoor environment. Whether it is the local park, or even a small back garden, the opportunities are as big as your child's imagination.

Building forts or go-karts with wood and small hand tools, gardening using wheelbarrows and spades, buckets of water for mixing, or mud pie making. The possibilities are endless.

I remember my children loving the game *The Ground is Lava* when they were young. They pretended the grass was made of lava so they could not step on it, but they had to keep moving around the garden. They played for hours setting up all sorts of obstacles they could jump from to avoid stepping on the lava. The game went on for ages as they navigated their way around the various structures! I am sure many of us have similar childhood memories. We shouldn't let the weather hold us back either. Instead encourage our children to get outside in all weathers. Remember the old Norwegian saying, "There is no bad weather only inadequate clothing!"

It Takes a Village:

One of my boys spent a morning at the beach with me recently. The weather was awful. It was raining constantly. We were soaked to the bone, but we embraced it all! We really enjoyed the silly little moments, collecting shells and stones. As we left the beach to return home he turned to me and said "Mammy, this is the best time I ever had with you." This guy loves his gadgets etc, but nature really is the best medicine in the eyes of a nine year old!

[Credit: Jane Foden via Facebook]

👍 Give it a Try!

- The overall message when aiming to support our children to become confident explorers is that as they master new skills, take on new responsibilities, and try new things, their confidence in their own abilities grows.
- We need to give our children opportunities to take responsibility for tasks, and to take healthy risks. As parents we need to allow our children to face challenges and become independent thinkers.
- Of course, we want to support our children, and want them to succeed in life, but try to put away that lawnmower or helicopter! Stand back and allow your children to face the obstacles in their lives.
- Instead of trying to micromanage, save your involvement for the times when they really need it. This will give them the confidence to approach life independently, knowing that you are always there in the background if they need to call on you.

CHAPTER 3

MOVING MOUNTAINS –
SELF ESTEEM AND RESILIENCE

It is easier to build strong children than to repair broken men.
Frederick Douglass

What is Self-Esteem?

Self-esteem is the foundation on which so much of our children's lives are built. It impacts on our thinking, which makes a difference to how we view the world and our place within it. It can influence the decisions we make about our lives, and whether we reach our full potential. It involves how we see ourselves and perceive our value. It is what we think, feel, and believe about ourselves.

In terms of the impact of self-esteem, children with good self-esteem tend to have better relationships with others. They do not feel the need to belittle themselves or others. There is no need to put anyone else down to elevate themselves. Instead, they usually have an awareness and acceptance of their own strengths and weaknesses, which can make their journey through life easier.

For me, good self-esteem involves two important aspects. They are our feelings of capability combined with our sense of being loved. We need both aspects to have a realistic but positive view of our self-worth. Our capability helps us feel strong enough to rise to the challenges we may face in life. It is not a sense of entitlement, arrogance, or a feeling you can do no wrong. It is about knowing yourself and believing you are worthy of success.

In terms of being loved, parents who go to parenting talks and buy parenting books, have the love aspect sorted. They may feel flawed, or that their parenting could be further developed, but the love and connection is there. But capability is an area that needs continuing growth throughout our lives.

Sometimes we worry that by encouraging self-belief we will give our children an inflated sense of self-worth. We may know adults or children whose self-esteem appears inflated, coming across as a sense of entitlement. In adults we often link this to narcissism, and it is not something we want for our children. Bear in mind, this is not true of self-esteem which comes from a belief in our true value and worth as an individual. There is a danger that if a child is praised for every little thing they do, whether the praise is deserved or not, they may end up with an over-inflated view of themselves. This usually leads to difficulties for the child if their peers do not appreciate this sense of superiority.

We also don't want our children to base their view of themselves on the judgements of others, or to constantly need validation from others. Instead we are looking for the middle ground. We want our children to have a stable sense of self-worth. We want them to understand how their individual talents can be developed throughout their lives. For this reason, it is important when considering self-esteem to also consider self-compassion and a growth mindset.

From the Horse's Mouth

I remember watching a four-year-old girl on her first day in playschool. This lovely little child struggled to make friends, as the rest of the children in the group had already made alliances and she found it difficult to break through. It was heartbreaking to watch her attempts to forge friendships and face rejection. You could visibly see her deflate as she struggled to connect with the other children. Although you could see her confidence take a little dip, that evening she went home and regrouped. The following day she came back into the setting, armed with ideas for play, and soon approached a little boy. It was like watching a fisherman cast out his rod and reel in a fish! She soon had a very willing playmate. But what really struck me was that this little lady did not take the initial rejection personally. Yes, it dented her confidence, but instead of believing she was not a worthy playmate, she focused on ideas to help her make friends. When you are four, coming up with great games to play is an amazingly effective way to build relationships! I am always reminded of this little girl when I think of a child with good self-esteem and resilience. She knew instinctively that she was still worthy of friendship. She just had to find a way to show the other children that this was the case!

When our self-esteem is high, we believe we are strong enough to meet the challenges we face in life. When it is low, we do not fully appreciate our value. Importantly, it is not something which is set in stone, instead it develops out of our interactions. As parents, it is something we can support and help grow.

What is Resilience?

Intricately linked to the area of self-esteem is the concept of resilience which is often referred to as the ability to bounce back from difficulties. I always believe when we use the term bounce back that it doesn't accurately represent resilience. Resilience is more about clawing your way back from difficult situations - the ability to recover from stress. When we are at our lowest, resilience is what keeps us plodding on.

As parents we are often tempted to swoop in and rescue our children from all adversity. Yet, as we discussed earlier, some challenges can help our children to develop the skills they need to flourish. We become resilient by picking ourselves up from failure, dusting ourselves off, and trying again. It is not something we automatically have or don't have. It is something we continue to develop throughout our lives.

> *Parents are one of the most important influences on children's resilience. There will be times when we cannot influence the stress they are under, but we can help them to develop coping skills to build their resilience.*

We all experience setbacks and loss at points in our lives. We feel sad sometimes, and that is fine, but we need to learn through experience that we can pick ourselves up and carry on. Our children need to know they can cope during these challenging periods.

Resilient children also appear to have more advanced problem-solving and decision-making skills. Again, this is very much linked to the area of self-esteem, which involves a belief that you can control your destiny. These children maintain a high level of confidence and a realistic sense of control, which are important coping skills when faced with difficulties. When children feel confident and capable, it helps them to respond to problems with resilience. They keep trying even when things are difficult and are more likely to end up feeling a sense of accomplishment. These little triumphs give children the courage to handle new challenges, which is a positive cycle.

One of the most important things to remember about self-esteem and resilience from a parent's perspective is that neither concept is fixed. They can develop over time. And yet, neither concept is something we can simply provide for our children. Both are something they need to develop themselves. Our role is to support and scaffold them in that journey. There are five areas which I recommend parents focus on when supporting children's self-esteem and resilience. These are:

- Encourage independence
- Make time to listen
- Problem solving and decision making
- Praise for effort
- Growth mindset

We have already looked at independence in detail in Chapter 2, so I will deal with each of the other areas separately below.

Time to Listen

We know that the quality of the parent-child relationship is of vital importance for children's future mental health. A secure base is needed to foster healthy attachments, and from these attachments our children can blossom. Research has confirmed that even in the most at-risk children, an emotionally strong early attachment, ideally with a parent, acts as a long-term buffer against life stressors. This is particularly true for our children's self-esteem and resilience. To become strong in these areas, a child needs affirmation from at least one adult who makes them feel special and appreciated.

Learning from Psychology

Stephen Covey, author of *The Seven Habits of Highly Effective People*[8], popularised an old story about setting priorities. The story goes that a professor takes out a one-gallon mason jar and sets it on his desk in front of his class. He then proceeds to fill the jar up to the top with large rocks and asks his class if the jar is full. The class responds yes. He then takes out a bowl of pebbles and pours them into the jar. The pebbles settle into the spaces between the big rocks, and again he asks the class if the jar is full, to which they respond yes. The professor then takes out a bucket of sand and pours it into the jar until it fills all the spaces between the rocks and pebbles. Only then is the jar full.

The message is that if they had put the sand in first there would have been no room for the rocks or pebbles. Covey uses this demonstration to highlight the tasks of varying importance in the workday, including major goals, short term goals, and minor tasks. We can also apply this metaphor to our home lives. The rocks are equivalent to the most important things in our lives. For most of us, these are people - our children, close family, and friends. If everything else in that jar was reduced, these are the things that really give meaning to our lives. The pebbles are also important, perhaps our job and hobbies, but they are not as meaningful. The sand represents the mundane tasks that take up so much of our day, and they are often the things we give priority to. If the big rocks are the most important things in our lives, including our children, we need to make sure we prioritise time with them or else they may not fit into the jar.

This is something I think many of us struggle with - ensuring we have quality time with our children. It is worth considering how we can ensure our personal 'rocks' are given priority. It is also worth noting that it is not always in our best interests to cram in as many pebbles and sand as we can. Sometimes we need a bit of space between those big rocks. Space to have some calm in our lives, time for reflection, and time to breathe.

To ensure we have real time for connection, it can help to set aside time as often as you can for one-on-one time with each of your children. This can be done in different ways for each child.

For some children, we don't actively have to try to work in time. These are the children who make sure they get our undivided attention during the day! But each child is different, and it is important to consider the different ways we can connect with each one. For some it might be bedtime as we wind down at the end of the day. Relaxed and snuggled in together can be a great time to ask about their day. For other children, we may need to work harder to make sure we have one on one time. For example, it could be when walking side by side without eye contact. These children are more likely to open up when there is no pressure to connect. It is about finding what works for you and your child. But whatever works for you, give them your full undivided attention.

There are about 940 Saturdays between the day your child is born and the day they go to college. If your child is now five years old, you have used up 260 of them!

This does not need to involve taking part in expensive experiences for our children. Everyday activities provide unplanned, unstructured moments of social interaction that are all important for positive relationship building. Spending time with each child, focused one-on-one with them, and letting them know you love spending time with them will help support their self-esteem. I am not saying it is always easy to find time, for example when you have a new baby it can be hard to find individual time for older siblings. But take comfort from the fact that research shows it is *quality* of interactions, not *quantity*, that is important.

 From the Horse's Mouth

I can usually find opportunities to connect with my daughters, but I have always had to work to find ways to connect with my son. He was always one of those children who when asked what he had done in school that day would reply, "Nothing!" Driving in the car is the one place I found worked for us to talk. From when he was little, trapped in his car seat, with me keeping an eye in the rear-view mirror, I found if he was sitting in the car, he was more likely to open up to me. He didn't have to make eye contact, I could keep an eye on him, and he was more likely to respond to my questions. To this day I take every opportunity for a drive with him whenever I can. I must be the only mother in Ireland who had a pang of regret when their child passed his driving test! Driving was the time I found out so much about what was happening in his life.

The overall message is to make sure we prioritise some time for each of our children. Time when we give them our full attention, time to listen and reconnect. Remember these moments of connection not only support our child's development, but they are also the moments which are essential to us as parents. Slowing down, listening to our children, and fully focusing on that relationship reminds us of what is important in life.

 It Takes a Village

My 8-year-old son James has been begging me to get into the inflatable pool out the back with him for two days. Yesterday evening, not hot or warm, I donned my togs in my 10-month post baby figure and got in. My frowning and looks of disgust when he splashed me or begged me to get under the water were awful, but he just wanted me to have fun with him. Last night I looked at the photographic evidence on my husband's phone. I just zoned in on his face. My heart melted. Bless him. You could see it meant the world to him. It made me feel so glad I got in and yet bad I hadn't sooner. They really do just want you to stop a moment and jump into their world.

[Credit: Gráinne Dunne via Facebook]

When we are spending this quality time with our children, we want to be the adult that reminds them of their strengths. Letting them know we value their unique characteristics is another important aspect of building self-esteem. As part of this we need to consider the emphasis we put on different skills and dispositions. When our children are babies and at preschool, we tend to view the child holistically. We make clear that we value kindness, empathy, and consideration of others (what we traditionally refer to as the soft skills) as much as we value academics. When our children start primary school, and particularly when they get to the stage of completing Friday tests such as spellings, tables tests etc, we tend to shift towards rewarding academics rather than these other skills. If a child is academic, they are openly rewarded by the school system and by their peers. The responses of others make them very aware that their skills in these areas are valued.

The same can be said for children who are very sporty. All the children at training know who will be picked to play on the team for every match. They also know who will probably only get five minutes of play. No matter if a parent says, "It's not the winning, it's the taking part that counts," they are very aware that the child who scores all the goals is admired by everyone on the team. For children who may not be the strongest in the class academically, or who may not often make the sports team, it is important we make clear that we value their individual strengths equally.

👍 Give it a Try!

If they are artistic, display their art. If they are musical, give them every opportunity to show and develop their talent. Make sure your child sees you value qualities such as kindness, empathy, generosity, sense of humour, and sensitivity to the needs of others. These are just as important as academics and sporting prowess, and, later in life, may well be the skills and dispositions which really count.

Remember as well as this one-on-one time with each child, positive family time also strengthens our connection. For most of us, it takes some planning and prioritising to make sure we have these quality family experiences. Some of the strategies we can use to try make this happen are:

- have dinner as a family as often as you can
- have family popcorn and movie nights
- have family board game or card game nights
- all cook a special dinner together

- take up shared hobbies
- visit parks or beaches together

The key is to pick ideas which work for you and your family, and soon you will find these small steps to building lasting bonds are second nature to you.

Problem Solving

Developing our children's skills in problem solving and decision-making has an equally crucial effect on building self-esteem and resilience. The most important way we can do this is to try not solve all their problems for them. This sounds easy, but in reality it is hard for most of us.

As a loving parent there is a temptation to protect our children any time we feel they are at risk. However, you can help build self-esteem and resilience by aiding your children in developing problem-solving skills so they can independently resolve difficulties. You want them to prove to themselves that when things go wrong, they can cope. They need to learn this, and practice it, for themselves.

One of the earliest ways we do this is by giving choices to our children. These choices help to set the foundation for a feeling of control over their life.

 Learning from Psychology

In psychology we speak about *locus of control*, a concept developed by psychologist Julian Rutter which refers to our assumptions about the control we have over life events. It is divided into two types, internal and external. If a child has a primarily internal locus of control this means they believe they have personal control over events in their life. They feel their success is related to their own efforts. If their locus of control is primarily external, they feel their life is governed by external factors, and they have limited control over events. This can lead to a feeling of helplessness. Locus of control develops over childhood, but children who are encouraged to take responsibility for their lives, even by making small decisions, are more likely to learn they have control over their world.

Giving children limited choices can be the start of giving children some autonomy over their lives, allowing them to take part in decision making. Little things, like giving your child a choice between two options, for example, would you like peas or carrots with your dinner? Or a choice of how many, for example, would you like two or three pieces of apple on your plate? It could be a choice between two people, for example, would you like mum or dad to put you to bed tonight? I often say to parents one of the best ways to allow children to start to have control is by deciding what they will wear to preschool. I can see the horrified faces of parents as I mention this at talks! I try to reassure them that I don't mean giving free reign to the child to pull out every piece of clothing in their wardrobe each morning. But our toddlers have truly little control over their worlds, and to choose between two outfits for preschool can give them good foundations for decision making. This will help them to develop confidence in their own ability to make good decisions.

As well as control, the skills of problem solving are important to develop. Parents supporting from the sidelines instead of solving problems for them, is key to enabling this to happen. When a problem arises, discuss options. We want our children to come to understand there are always options.

Little ones may have difficulty thinking of possible solutions to problems, so encourage them to consider potential answers. Help them come up with ideas and support them in making choices. For example, if your child is having difficulty with her best friend in school, you can ask her to think about a couple of ways of solving the situation. Help her reflect upon these possible solutions. She might think the best answer is for you to phone her friend's mother and demand she play with her. OK, that is one possible option, although you will probably have no intention of taking her up on this choice! But there is always more than one option. She might suggest you call the teacher and ask her to tell her friend she must play with her. OK, that is another possible solution. Or she might speak to the teacher and ask her to fix the problem. If she can think of no more, you can suggest a few. Maybe she could speak to her friend and tell her she has hurt her feelings? Maybe she might need a little space from her friend and should play with someone else for a while?

Let her reflect on the options and consider which one she could try. If she makes the decision that she wants to tell the teacher and see if she can fix the problem, you can ask her if she is sure one of the other options might not be worth a try first. If she insists that this is her preferred option, even though you might not agree, let her give it a try. She will probably find that the teacher will ask her to speak to her friend herself and see if she can solve the issue. But your daughter will learn from this. It will give her an insight into the decision-making process and the consequences of her decisions.

👍 Give it a Try!

Introducing young children to the basics of problem solving:

- Listen while the child explains the problem.
- Repeat it back to the child to make sure you have understood correctly.
- Ask the child to identify any possible solutions. Remember they don't have to be perfect solutions!
- If necessary, expand on these solutions with some ideas of your own. You want them to see there are always many options.
- Reflect with the child all the possible solutions, evaluate the possible positive or negative outcomes and narrow them down.
- Allow the child to choose the solution they want to try.

Going through this problem-solving process is helping your child develop the building blocks for good decision making for when they are older. You want them to get used to always considering different options when faced with a problem rather than feeling helpless and needing to seek out others for help.

🔍 What Does the Research Say?

A minor change in thinking can really help with this. Very often when we are faced with a problem, we start to think about what we *should* do to try to solve it. Instead, try to reframe it as thinking about what we *could* do.

Research from the Harvard Business School[9] found that when we try to solve problems considering what we *should* do, it tricks our minds and narrows our focus into searching for one solution. Whereas if we change our language, and consider what we *could* do, it opens our minds up to looking for multiple possibilities. We are more likely to consider a wider range of more imaginative solutions.

They use the example of the pilot of the plane which landed on the Hudson River in New York in 2009 to highlight this point. Shortly after taking off, his plane lost both engines, and he had to make an emergency decision about what to do. The "what *should* I do" response was to try to land at the nearest airport runway. Instead, he allowed himself to think about what he *could* do, and landed on the Hudson River, saving the lives of all aboard. The point is he did not allow himself to be constrained by the textbook response but considered all possible options. This is the type of thinking we want to encourage in our children. The hope is that this approach becomes a learned behavior, and when they are older this will be their go-to method for decision making.

How we frame the problem is also something we need to consider when facing a dilemma. If our children see problems as external to them, then they can work on developing strategies to solve the issue. Too often our children generalise about themselves when faced with difficulties. For example, one day they are struggling to learn their times tables in school, then they decide they are no good at math, and next thing they have moved on to telling themselves they are stupid (oh, how I hate that word). It is important they understand that the problem isn't within them. The problem is external, it is something they are struggling to deal with, but there are always strategies which can be put in place to help. So, for that example, we can acknowledge that tables are hard to learn. Are there tips or tricks we can use to help make it easier to learn them? One trick could be singing the tables along to a tune to make learning them easier. Another could be to use your fingers to help work out some of the times tables. The point is we are framing the problem as being something external which we need support with.

What happens if they make a poor decision, or fail in some way? If they make a poor decision and face difficult consequences, it is even more important not to swoop in and rescue them! If your child decides the best solution in the best friend scenario is to ask the teacher to solve the problem for them, we need to let them follow through on their own decisions in order to learn (provided we know they will come to no real harm in making that decision). The fear of making mistakes can be an obstacle to developing good self-esteem and resilience. Instead of avoiding any task or decision which could lead to error, encourage them to remember that mistakes are an important part of learning and growing.

It's vital to ensure your child knows you love her even when she fails or makes bad decisions. You can also get them to reflect after an event, on how they might approach it differently in hindsight. In order to really learn from their mistakes, they need to reflect on them. It can also help to talk to them about your past mistakes, the consequences, and how you learned from them. We want them to understand that making mistakes is how we learn to expand our problem-solving skills and foster perseverance. They help us to cultivate stronger judgement and find new ways of looking at the world. Helping them to focus on effort rather than outcome can also be useful to support perseverance and resolve.

Praise for Effort

As I said earlier, an important component of self-esteem is feeling competent. A child may feel loved, but if they are hesitant about their own abilities, they can have low self-esteem. When our children achieve something, they get a sense of themselves as strong and capable and this gives them confidence to take on new tasks. An important aspect of praise is to make sure we respond with excitement when our children accomplish a new skill or achieve a goal.

 From the Horse's Mouth

When my eldest daughter was about three or four months old, lying under her baby gym, she recognised for the first time she had moved one of the toys. I was watching her and saw the realisation on her face that it was her hand that caused the toy to move. She had begun to understand she could control the movement, and instead of randomly striking the toys, she began to intentionally try to cause the movement again. Along with her understanding, I responded with praise and delight at this achievement. Not only did she have the satisfaction of knowing she could cause the object to move, but she was also delighting in my excited response to her developing hand-eye coordination.

Another example I always think of is when we are toilet training our children. How often have you seen a child parade a filled potty to adoring adults who respond with excitement and cheers at the contents! We are so aware of responding with excitement when our young children achieve their developmental milestones. As they grow older an important way to support our children in developing a sense of their own worth and capability is to praise them for the effort they put into a task instead of praising them only for the finished product. We should aim to reward effort as well as outcome.

Learning from Psychology

Behaviourist Psychologist B.F. Skinner developed a method of learning called *Operant Conditioning* based on a system of rewards and punishments. It is a technique based on the idea that behaviour which is rewarded is likely to be repeated, and is often used to teach animals, and sometimes children. The technique involves breaking tasks down into small steps and rewarding children for completing each task. It is quite an effective tool as it teaches the child to expect a reward in exchange for the behaviour. However, one danger of using this technique is that the child then expects to be rewarded every time they behave that way, so they become reliant on receiving a reward. In this way, it undermines the child's intrinsic motivation, their own enthusiasm for working hard and learning the task.

We want our children to work hard at things because they want to do well, and it makes them feel strong and capable, not just to get a reward from us.

This is one of the reasons I hate to see star charts for academics in the school system. Although I can see a benefit in using them at times such as toilet training, for academics their use concerns me. Within any given classroom you will have some children who will gain a star each week for their spellings, times tables, and so on, without having put any effort into learning them. While other children can put huge effort into learning their spellings and tables but may never get them all right. They will struggle to gain stars, and the message these children are receiving is damaging. Although using rewards can be effective when linked to attainment, praise for effort is more effective than tangible rewards (such as stars) which can diminish intrinsic motivation.

From the Horse's Mouth

One of my daughters attended a preschool which I was not particularly happy with. She would bring home photocopied templates which the children were given to colour in. At Christmas it could be Santa's face, at Halloween a pumpkin. She never took any interest in showing me these sheets or having them put up for display. In education we often call sheets like this "refrigerator art" as they are sent home purely for display on the fridge! I noticed how, in these pictures, my daughter would colour within the lines, while at home she would never do this. When I asked her about it she told me, "Oh, teacher did that for me!" I thought to myself, these pictures should be on the teacher's fridge not mine, as it was the teacher who had coloured them! These pictures were being undertaken so an end product could be sent home to parents, rather than as a joyful educational experience for the child.

I moved her to a new preschool and one of the things I loved when I visited this preschool was a row of easels with paint and paper where children could paint any time they wanted. My daughter would come home every day with lots of A3 sheets of brown paint! Many of them had a hole in the middle where she painted right through the paper! When I asked her about them, she joyfully told me, "First I painted yellow, then red, then green…" She took pride in telling me all about her work. I could almost picture her, arms spread, slathering all the paint onto her sheet. These were very much hers and she took pride in the effort that had gone into making them.

When they have put a lot of effort into a task, we can say something like, "I love this picture you have made for me. I can tell you worked so hard on it." Or, "Oh wow, you should be so proud of all the work you put into that picture." It is also important in our praise to be truthful in our responses. "Good job" does not clearly tell your child what you are proud of. "I really like the way you used so many different colours in your picture," is more specific.

Fixed and Growth Mindset

Reminding our children that we are proud of the effort they have put into a task cultivates growth. As does reminding them that we are proud of the strategies they have used. We are proud of the focus and perseverance they gave to a task. This will help our children to develop what we call a growth mindset and become more resilient. It will remind them that their beliefs about how they approach the world can lead them to a new perspective on life. They should know they are a work in progress. Every time they push themselves outside of their comfort zone and take on a new task or challenge, new connections are forming in their brains based on these experiences.

The concept of growth mindset was developed by Carol Dweck and is outlined in her book *Mindset: The New Psychology of Success*. She studied children's beliefs about intelligence and their motivation to learn. She found that children with what she called a "fixed mindset" believe their intelligence is fixed, and as such will avoid challenges which they feel they may not achieve. They also see no need to work to improve intelligence and ability as they feel these are set in stone. Those with a "growth mindset" believe intelligence and ability can be developed through hard work. Basically, these children believe people can grow and change, and that effort will result in improvement. Because of this, they are more likely to persist with challenges. They accept that failure is a part of learning, will take on challenging tasks and will put in time and effort to learn new things. Dweck argues that it is not our children's natural ability or talent which brings success, it is whether they approach the world with a fixed or growth mindset.

Although children can have different mindsets in various areas, most children have a general tendency towards one mindset or the other. This is the reason praising intelligence or ability will never foster self-esteem. In fact, it can jeopardise the chance of success!

🔍 What Does the Research Say?

Although mindsets are relatively stable, research has shown they can be altered by educational interventions. One study on growth mindset[10] involved dividing children into two groups, each of which took part in a different workshop on the brain. The first group were taught about the different stages of memory. The second group were taught about the plasticity of the brain – its potential to change and adapt as we learn. Students at the workshop explaining how intelligence could be developed, were more likely to report after the session that working hard was necessary to achieve. Three times as many students in this group showed an increase in effort and motivation than the fixed mindset group, which impacted on their academic performance.

Nearly two years later, they were still outperforming the group with a more fixed theory of intelligence, meaning even a very brief intervention such as this was proven to have long-lasting impact on the student's motivation and achievement. This reminds us of the importance of our children's understanding that their brain is developing all the time.

We know from such studies that praise is closely connected to how our children view their intelligence. If children are constantly praised for being naturally talented or clever, there is a danger they will develop a fixed mindset. Instead, when we praise hard work and effort, it cultivates a growth mindset.

The Science Bit!

Recent neurological research on the brain confirms that mistakes are opportunities for learning[11]. In fact, mistakes are times when our brain connections grow. When studying the neural connections in brains, researchers found that when people make mistakes, electrical signals, called synapses, fire. A signal is sent to ensure that conscious attention is given to the mistake. The brain is challenged to cope with the error, which increases electrical activity, and this results in growth!

The message is clear, we need to encourage children to think of their brain as something that is strengthened with use. As we try new experiences some connections are strengthened, and some are eliminated. We can encourage our children to try new things, make mistakes, and try again, knowing that their brains can change and adapt because of these different experiences.

 Top Tip!

Next time your child says they can't do something, whether it is their math homework, riding their bike, or learning a new sport, try adding the word yet! Instead of, "I can't do this," we have, "I can't do this yet." This small word can be immensely powerful as it helps our children to understand that they are on a learning curve. It reminds them that they live in a world filled with possibilities. It gives them the power to grow and learn and have confidence for the future.

Bear in mind, this idea about growth mindset also applies to us as parents! Instead of seeking perfection, adopting a mindset of growth and learning helps us to build connected families. Seeing past our mistakes and our current challenges are like stepping-stones for growth. Good parenting skills are learned, they improve with effort, and our relationships with our children are always developing. If we try to see both ourselves and our children as a work in progress, it reminds us that the whole family has potential for growth. As parents, the challenge for us is to give our children a love of learning, to teach them to put in the effort and face new encounters without fear of failure. This will help them to develop and build their own self-esteem. The mistakes we make as parents along the way help show our children that learning is a lifelong process.

Kindness and Self-Compassion

Becoming involved in constructive experiences, and activities which encourage cooperation rather than competition, are especially helpful in terms of our children's views of themselves within the world. Opportunities for our children to help others are as good for them as they are for the children they are helping.

Sharing with younger siblings can be a great way to foster co-operation, for example, older ones reading to little ones. Involving them in activities where they are giving their time and effort in doing something for others is also helpful. My youngest has volunteered with the Team Hope Christmas Shoebox Appeal since she was a child. Her involvement has increased each year, and by September she usually has a little shoebox factory set up in our spare room! This gives her a good understanding of the difference you can make by taking time out to do something for others.

From the Horse's Mouth

Children seem to have an inborn need to help others. I remember when I was observing a Junior Infant classroom during my PhD research, I was struck by the delight the children took in taking on jobs for the teacher. One of the less glamorous jobs was the bins. There were three bins in the classroom, general rubbish, recyclables, and the bin for food waste. The food waste was not the most pleasant bin, but every day, the absolute delight on the faces of the children given the task of carrying this manky bin around to gather the waste food made me smile to myself. I have memories of beaming faces telling me, "I'm on the bin today Mary!" It reminded me how much our children love to be helpers. Providing opportunities for them to help is a very concrete way of highlighting that they have something to contribute to their world.

Self-compassion is the extension of kindness, understanding, and care towards ourselves. When faced with our own mistakes and failures, self-compassion affords us the same grace when we are struggling that we would give to our loved ones. Making sure our children show kindness and compassion to themselves as well as others can support their own self-esteem. We are all growing. We are all learning. Each one of us is a work in progress. Life is made up of both highs and lows, and during their childhood and indeed their lifetime, our children will experience both aspects.

In order to develop resilience, they need to practice self-compassion when things go wrong. This is not the same as telling our children to cheer up.

There is nothing more guaranteed not to cheer someone up than being told to cheer up!

It is not about putting on a false sense of positivity. It is about developing an awareness of these negative emotions and being kind to ourselves when we are feeling this way, thereby allowing the emotion to shift. It is about recognising feelings, helping our children label their feelings, and finding a safe way to express them.

For children, our actions speak louder than our words and we serve as one of their first role models. Ensuring we are a positive role model for our children has quite a big effect on growing our children's self-esteem. It is an Irish affliction to have difficulty accepting a compliment. We have all heard the old joke, someone tells us we look nice, and what do we say, "Thanks hun, Penneys!" When someone pays you a compliment, you should try to say thank you and nothing else. No if's or but's, just thanks.

It really is worth considering the messages we give our children when we cannot accept a compliment. Imagine you and your son have spent the evening making cupcakes to take to a cake sale in the school. You make them all and decorate them beautifully. As you arrive at the school, someone compliments them, and you say, "Oh no, it's nothing. Just something we threw together last night." You are telling your child that you place no value on the effort you have put in, and that you are not proud of what you achieved. I think we can all be guilty of this at times, and no matter how much we tell our children to value the effort they have put into a task, we need to show them that we place value on ourselves.

If we are very self-critical, we are modelling the behaviour which is the opposite of our goals for our children. In today's fast paced world, it seems we are used to being hard on ourselves, and rarely think of showing ourselves kindness. We often feel alone when we experience the hardships of life, but the struggles of life are part of our shared experience. It can help to put our problems into perspective if we acknowledge we are not alone in them. Others have similar experiences.

👍 Give it a Try!

- Spend quality time communicating with your children, giving them your undivided attention, and highlighting their individual strengths.

- Provide choices for your child. These beginning choices help to set the foundation for a feeling of control over one's life.

- When faced with problems encourage your child to consider as many possible solutions as they can think of, evaluate each one, and decide which one they will try out.

- Praise your child for effort and persistence over outcome. Try to give honest and accurate feedback.

- Remind your child that mistakes are an important part of learning, just because they can't do something now, it simply means they can't do it yet.

CHAPTER 4

BEST FRIENDS FOREVER - CHILDREN'S FRIENDSHIPS

The only way to have a friend, is to be one.
Ralph Waldo Emerson

The Importance of Friendships

Good friendships can have a huge developmental influence on our children. They benefit both social and emotional development while boosting happiness and wellbeing. Research shows friendships help our children develop dispositions such as self-esteem and confidence, while also assisting them to deal with conflict and adversity. They increase a child's sense of belonging and help them to cope with life's stresses and transitions. Having a hand to hold as you face life's challenges is a great support both physically and metaphorically.

Friendships can be an inoculation against life's difficulties, providing our children with support and comfort at times of trouble. They can also, of course, be the cause of heartbreak and pain.

Friendship skills don't come automatically to all children. Knowing how to make friends and maintain relationships involves many different skill sets. For some children this ability comes naturally, however for others managing the world of friendships is harder to navigate. We can support our children in developing friendships, teaching them the competencies which will help them to be a good friend, and how to cope when friendships become challenging.

Friendships Through the Years

Children's friendships take different forms at different ages. Toddlers usually start side by side in parallel play where they may seem to be working together at a task but there is little interaction between the two children. At this age, children can have difficulty sharing and co-operating, but their social skills are starting to develop. They often learn by imitation.

Pre-schoolers engage in more interaction with others and friendships start to develop at this age, although, friends are usually based on availability. Every child they interact with positively is considered a friend. They might introduce you to a child they met five minutes earlier as, "my friend Michael."

 Learning from Psychology

Jean Piaget (1896-1980) is perhaps the greatest influence on modern child psychology. He made a key contribution to the area of developmental psychology, particularly in the area of children's understanding of the world. He believed children up to about the age of seven have difficulty reflecting on other people's perception of the world. They are egocentric, which means they tend to only see the world from their own viewpoint. Following on from his work, it is widely accepted that our young children have difficulty seeing the perspective of others. This is not very helpful when developing friendships!

As children get older and continue to develop socially, for example developing communication skills and cooperation, their friendships also become deeper. Their understanding of relationships is developing, and you will sometimes hear a school aged child use friendship as a bargaining tool. They also tend to see another child as a friend based on whether they do nice things for them. You may have noticed that most primary school teachers change seating plans regularly so the students get to know everyone in their class. By doing this, children learn you don't have to be best friends with everyone, and it helps them to deal with different personalities.

From about age eight up to the age of twelve, friendships become stronger. Children of this age are better at taking the perspective of others. This means they have a greater awareness of their friends' feelings. But this is the time when jealousies are also more likely to start as children have a stronger sense of fairness and the rules of friendship. This can also be the time of secret clubs, with lots of discussion about who should be included, and the rules of the club.

As children get older, they place a much higher value on emotional closeness with friends, with an emphasis on trust and support within friendships. These relationships help them to learn about themselves as they often get more honest feedback from a friend than they do from family. Close friendships also help our older children foster the skills for healthy adult relationships: kindness, empathy, the ability to listen and console. The process of arguing and making up is also developing during the ins and outs of these peer relationships. In terms of supporting friendships, talking to them about the use of empathy when considering the perspectives of others can be effective, which we will consider in more depth below.

Parental Intervention

In many ways when our children are young, we determine their social circle. We also tend to interfere in their friendships! We don't allow children out to play in the same way our parents did, meaning the opportunity to meet friends 'out on the road' is limited. Instead, we are more likely to have scheduled play dates. As much as we would like our children to become best friends with the children we choose, child friendships need to develop on their terms, not ours. When we intervene or manage these relationships, we're not allowing them to learn and grow. Instead, we can stand back and allow them to learn how friendships work.

As an alternative to socially engineering every activity for our children to make sure they will have a friend available, we can encourage them to approach new experiences alone occasionally. Children often surprise us with how capable they are at making connections with others if we step back and allow them to do so at their own pace. If your child is struggling to make friendships, you can of course support them by arranging opportunities for them to mix socially, but also step back so they can learn social skills.

Friendship skills

In order to develop strong relationships a child needs
to know what they want and expect from a friendship.
But what is a real friend?

The definition of a friend is different from person to person, but we know that a friend is someone who is there for you if you really need them. Someone who shows loyalty to you, and who values your friendship in return. They make it clear by their words and their actions that they like you and are a support to you.

What is a Friend? Sesame Street[12] tells our children that a friend is someone to play with. Someone to share your toys with. Someone to tell stories with. Someone to go to the park with. Someone to laugh and joke with. Someone you would give up your last cookie for!

You may find that your child desperately wants to be accepted into the most popular group in his class, but does he actually share any interests with that group? If not, he might find it very difficult to be accepted. Speak to your child about what makes a good friend, and the qualities of the different children in his class, in clubs he attends, and with neighbours. Friendships where children have some interests in common, or are similar in terms of their likes, usually work well.

In terms of developing friendships, it can help them to consider the social skills which help to form friendships (see the checklist below for some ideas). Being approachable, responding positively to others, being helpful and kind, all help our children begin developing friendships. Communication skills are important, both talking and listening to others. Support your children with skills to start conversations with other children. If they are struggling, give them some ideas for opening questions.

👍 Give it a Try!

Here are some ideas for friendship skills to consider with your child, which can be adapted for different age groups.

- Do I smile and introduce myself when meeting someone new?
- Do I ask questions to get to know others?
- Do I tell people a little bit about myself and my hobbies?
- Do I listen to others without interrupting?
- Do I share with others and play fairly?
- Do I speak calmly when I am upset with a friend?
- Do I include everyone in my friendship group?
- Do I speak nicely about my friends to others?
- Do I try to help my friends solve their problems?
- Do I invite others to join in my games?
- Do I treat others with kindness?

Using these skill sets as areas to consider can help you open a conversation with your child about what makes a good friend.

For young children, play skills are also important including being willing to take part in games and make suggestions for play. Children who have more developed friendship and play skills are more likely to be invited in by the group. Children who come with an idea or a suggestion which interests the group are also likely to be able to join. It also helps if a child can show some self-control. For example, turn-taking, being able to cooperate and share, are all helpful when friendships are developing. If your child always wants to have their own way, and always wants others to play their game, they are going to run into difficulties in maintaining friendships. Family games nights, or family card games can be a great way of introducing these skills. They also need to develop coping skills, being able to respond to disappointment in relationships without becoming overly distressed. We can help children develop these skills by giving some gentle coaching when children are struggling.

 What Does the Research Say?

Research by Stanford University has found that one of the best predictors of both social and academic development in later years was a child's social skills in third grade[13]. Prosocial behaviour such as co-operating, helping and sharing, had long term impact. The researchers also considered early academic success and found it did not result in later academic achievement in the same way. Similar research by Pennsylvania State University[14] found children who demonstrated good social skills at nursery-school age went on to be more successful in life. The children who were more socially competent (including the abilities to share, help others and resolve peer problems) fared better both socially and occupationally long term.

This research reminds us that social and emotional learning is just as important as academic ability, and development of these social skills should be supported throughout childhood. These findings have confirmed what myself and many others have long suspected to be true. These skills are correlated not only to success as children, but also to life success. They are the ones we need to invest in when it comes to parenting.

Complex Friendships

We know friendships are an integral part of growing up, and research has shown friendships increase our chances of being happy. Nevertheless, friendships can also be complex relationships. Although some children make a best friend early in life, for many these relationships ebb and flow and maintaining friendships can be a struggle. During my years answering parent queries both on the radio and on television, friendship is one of the areas which comes up time and time again. When a child struggles to make friends or to maintain friendships, this can be a cause of real heartbreak, for both child and parent.

If your child fights with one of their friends or is left out, encourage them to talk about what happened. Be warm and empathise with how tough it can be when we argue with friends. Avoid responding when angry. To see our children emotionally aching becomes an emotionally charged moment for us. It absolutely cuts to our heart to see them hurting which makes it hard not to over-react. But anger will most likely make the matter worse. Take a few deep breaths first and respond calmly while covering your own upset to your child.

You and your family are their safe space. Home is the place they go to when they need to regroup and lick their wounds. It is also the place where they heal. Knowing their parent is devastated or angry about the situation can make healing more difficult. Our children need reassurance they will get a calm but caring response from us when they share their hurts.

Top Tip!

The most important message to get across is that you love them and believe in them. They have handled difficult situations in the past and are strong enough to face this one too. Allow them to fully share their feelings, empathise but divert them away from endlessly going over the difficulty.

When both you and your child are in a calmer place, let them go back to consider how they can deal with or resolve any conflicts. This is not a time to tell them what to do, instead offer ideas only if needed. Sorting it out for them will not help build their resilience, independence or growth. The more you allow them to use their own problem-solving skills the more skilled they will become at negotiating future relationships.

 Top Tip!

A good question to ask them to consider is whether or not they like themselves when they are with a specific friend or group of friends. Can they truly be themselves when they are with this person? Painful as it might be, sometimes it is in their best interests to move on from a friendship and develop new relationships with more like-minded peers.

Thinking about our friendships in terms of what they bring out in us, can help us to see who we are genuinely comfortable with. It is important they find friends who bring out the best in them, people who like them for who they really are, quirks and all. Friends they can trust.

Toxic Friendships

A toxic friendship can be difficult to define, but these friends most definitely cause your child more worry than joy. Instead of enriching their lives, the friendship has an unequal power dynamic with your child left feeling vulnerable and insecure. I have found in my parenting work that issues with toxic friendships and relational aggression (an insidious type of bullying designed to maintain social status) are becoming more and more commonplace. These friendships usually start well, with kindness shown until trust has developed. The pattern of behaviour then changes, often ending up in sabotage, exclusion and manipulation. It includes power games which can involve gossiping about a child, giving them the silent treatment, and belittling them. Toxic friends usually behave well in adult company and are clever enough to covertly hide the psychological war they are waging. In private these relationships involve undermining your child and exerting social control over the group. These friendships can take a huge toll on your child's self-esteem and confidence.

> *The pain parents and children feel as children are exposed to destructive behaviour from friends or classmates seems to be increasing every year. If you have ever despaired at the pain your child is experiencing due to toxic friendships, please know you are not alone. The fallout caused by these negative interactions is becoming more and more common.*

Relational aggression used to be commonplace in the teenage years, but now it seems to be starting much younger. It is typically played out by school aged girls and although a lot of the research relates to girls, it applies just as well to your son and his friendships. Many of us as adults have also experienced this behaviour.

 Learning from Psychology

Relational aggression is the psychologist's name for what the rest of us call 'mean girls' behaviour, or straight-up 'bitchiness'. It is a pattern of behaviour typically played out by school-age girls, but it is not exclusive to them. In fact, where do they learn it if not from their adult role models? Adults are just more subtle about it.

Chances are you've experienced relational aggression. You know it when it happens to you. It's an emotional slap in the face and you often feel a sense of shame and confusion. What distinguishes relational aggression from just being mean, is that it focuses on damaging a person's sense of social place. I see it as using relationships as weapons.

[Credit: Linda Stade, Education Writer and Consultant[15]]

When our children undergo this experience, we can also see an element of conditional friendship at play. Children within the group know their inclusion depends on their willingness to accept this type of behaviour. Fear of exclusion makes children who would not necessarily deliberately engage in this sort of behaviour themselves accept the bad treatment of others. How do we help them to stand up to this peer pressure?

It Takes a Village

A friend of mine told me about a powerful lesson in her daughter's high school class. They were learning about the Salem Witch Trials and their teacher told them they were going to play a game.

"I'm going to come around and whisper to each of you whether you're a witch or a regular person," she told them. "Your goal is to build the largest group possible that does not have a witch in it. At the end, any group found to include a witch gets a failing grade."

The teens dove into grilling each other. One fairly large group formed, but most of the students broke into small, exclusive groups, turning away anyone they thought gave off even a hint of guilt.

"Okay," the teacher said. "You've got your groups. Time to find out which ones fail. All witches, please raise your hands." No one raised a hand. The kids were confused and told him he'd messed up the game.

"Did I? Was anyone in Salem an actual witch? Or did everyone just believe what they'd been told?"

And that is how you teach kids how easy it is to divide a community. Shunning, scapegoating, and dividing destroy far more than they protect.

We're all in this together.

[Credit: Ria D. Megnin, MSW, LSW, MA, via Facebook]

Psychotherapist Stella O'Malley addresses this issue in her book *Bully Proof Kids*. She reminds us of the role of upstanders, distracters and supporters in dealing with relational aggression, bullying and toxic relationships. She argues that we need to address the culture of bystanders. These are children who are aware of what is happening. These bystanders often report they had sympathy for the child but felt unable to act. She argues we need to encourage our children to become upstanders, the people who stand up for victims. She advocates for a culture where the position of the bystander is considered complicit in bullying. If the safety net of arguing that they were just a bystander is challenged, she believes our children will be pushed towards the role of upstander. Then, she argues, bullying will become a more manageable situation, instead of the epidemic it is today.

👍 Give it a Try!

O'Malley recommends two approaches which can help children stand up to bullies. The first is by being a *Distracter*. This is when a child can recognise an issue is brewing and distract participants away from it. Perhaps by changing the topic or introducing something new into the conversation. This is a skill adults often use themselves in situations of conflict. As adults we can tell our children this is a tool they can use and talk to them about how to distract from potential conflict.

The second approach she recommends is to encourage your child to be a *Supporter*. This is when one child supports another in a difficult situation by doing something as small as making eye contact. It shows the victim that the behaviour is seen and acknowledged. Showing empathy in this way makes a child under pressure aware that they are not alone.

Power Games and Exclusion

What if our child is the one doing the leaving out? We have to bear in mind that it is possible our child may be a bully or may deliberately exclude classmates. A very common scenario is when a child is intentionally left out of birthday party invitations, when the rest of the class are all invited. What message are we giving our children if we allow them to single out one child in the class and exclude them from an invitation?

If we want our children to become people who are kind, include rather than exclude, and who are respectful of others, they need to see us doing the same. We want to teach them about kindness and inclusion and help them to develop the skills of empathy. Demonstrating that caring and empathy are our core values can play an important part in doing this.

It can help if we look critically at our own behaviour. If we are engaging in unintentional exclusionary behaviour then our children will follow our lead. Instead, could we go out of our way to include that parent standing alone every day at the school gate? If we are in the park and we point out to our child a little one who is alone and looking for someone to play with, then we should also show our children that we are there with a smile and a friendly word with a parent who is in the same position. If our children hear us constantly criticising our friends behind their backs, we cannot expect them to treat their friends with kindness and understanding.

Instead we can show our children by our words and actions that friends lift each other up. In times of conflict or misunderstanding, we can show them that we give our friends the benefit of the doubt. We can make a point of talking about the great qualities our friends have. The distinct strengths of different friends, and how the various qualities impact on our relationships.

- *Erin is a great listener, where would I be without her listening ear?*
- *Michael has a great sense of humour. He always lifts me up when I am feeling low.*
- *Kira is so thoughtful. She always offers me great advice if I am feeling overwhelmed.*

If a friend is stressed, let them hear you wonder is there anything you could do to help. Show them how you help and support your friends and celebrate their successes and achievements.

Reminding our children to be kind and inclusive of others by talking to them about compassion and empathy is vital. Even if they do not particularly like everyone in their class, everyone has a right to be included. These conversations are an opportunity to remind them of the values and principles which are important to us in terms of inclusiveness, empathy, and kindness to others who may be more vulnerable than us. Encourage them to look out for others and be aware of children who might need the hand of friendship.

Empathy and Compassion

Kindness starts from an understanding that we all struggle at times, and central to the concept of kindness is empathy. Empathy is a model which refers to the cognitive and emotional reactions of any person to the experiences of another. It involves putting yourself in another person's shoes, showing compassion, and supporting others in a time of need.

The Science Bit!

From a developmental perspective, children start to show empathy from about two to three years old, when they are developing an understanding of the experiences of others. However, children from twelve months old have been found to demonstrate altruistic helpfulness such as comforting other children in distress and helping others in need. Even young infants are able to perceive and respond to the affective states of others. This suggests that these processes are hard-wired in the brain. Although emotional development continues through to adolescence, it seems we have a natural predisposition to develop empathy. However, as parents we can influence how, and to whom, our children express it.

Empathy can be a very important factor in developing friend-ships, as it gives us the ability to understand and share the thoughts or feelings of another person. We may not have experienced the same circumstances as that person, but empathy gives us a will-ingness to try to understand the impact of events on them, and their perspective on life events.

Empathy can be broken down into three categories. The first is emotional empathy. This is the ability to share the feelings of another person and helps us to build emotional connections with others. We are all born with emotional empathy. It is a natural response to the pain of another human. The second type is cog-nitive empathy or perspective taking which is simply knowing how the other person feels and what they might be thinking. This kind of empathy helps us to become better communicators. The third category is compassionate empathy also known as empathic concern. Psychologist Daniel Goleman in his book *Emotional Intelligence*, advises that this type of empathy is important as it goes beyond simply understanding the feelings of others. It moves us to respond and support the other person in whatever way we can. Both cognitive empathy and compassionate empathy can be learned. If our children are going to learn these skills, we need to teach them, but are we?

 What Does the Research Say?

Research has found that levels of empathy in students have declined dramatically over the past few decades. The Harvard Graduate School of Education[16] published some interesting findings about our children's empathy and the messages they receive from parents about kindness and empathy. This survey of 10,000 students found that a large majority valued personal success over concerns for others. The authors note that the root of the issue could be linked to a real difference between rhetoric and reality in terms of parental priorities. The teens responded that their parents were much more concerned with their achievement and personal happiness than caring for others. The authors note the irony of the findings is how this focus on achievement and personal happiness doesn't appear to increase either children's achievement or happiness. Children under pressure to achieve do not appear to outperform other students, and children who are protected from adversity do not appear to have the coping strategies important to long-term happiness.

It is clear, as parents, we should be focusing more on teaching our children to become caring, ethical citizens. If our children are lacking in empathy, some of the blame must lay with the adults in their lives and the messages they are receiving in society today. If we are so focused in modern society on academic achievement, we may be failing to fully nurture qualities like kindness and empathy. Our children may be hearing that we value these qualities, but they see individual achievement being rewarded to a greater extent. For example, peers being rewarded in school for academic achievement, or in extracurricular activities being rewarded for sporting prowess. No matter what we say, we are not demonstrating that caring and empathy are our core values. We need to not only talk the talk, but walk the walk. We can try to do this by reminding ourselves that our success as parents is not gauged by the achievements of our children, but by the type of person they become. Also, ensuring they are aware of how we notice and value these qualities is of great importance to their development of empathy.

 It Takes a Village

We could learn a lot about empathy by studying the approach taken in Danish schools. Denmark has been found to have the happiest people in the world almost every year since 1973. As compared to schools in many other countries, which focus on individualism and competition, in Danish schools the emphasis is on wellbeing. The curriculum has a strong focus on teamwork and building empathy rather than individual achievement. Learning and applying empathy is incorporated into the school curriculum in every class from preschool upwards. For example, *Klassens Time* is an hour every class spend each week talking as a group about any difficulties in relationships within the class or any problems they have as a group. They then come together to try to develop a collective solution to the problem. Any problem, whether personal or school related, is open for discussion, and the teacher guides the group in their considering of ideas which might help solve the problem. The Danes understand that in order to feel empathy, children need to not only take the perspective of the other person, but to appreciate that it has equal value and deserves the same respect as their own viewpoint. They may not agree with another student's opinion, however they recognise that each child has a right to be heard. In this way they seek to reach a solution based on real listening and real understanding. What an important lesson for our children!

Steps to Develop Empathy

In order to support a child in developing empathy, we need to model the behaviour we want them to follow. So, start by listening! When someone else is in difficulty, it can be tempting to jump in to help by interrupting them to share your similar experience, to offer advice, or suggest a solution. Instead, the core of empathy is to focus on understanding the situation, and how it makes the person feel. This is what we want our children to learn. Taking time to listen will give them a better understanding and enable them to connect with how that situation is making the person feel. Then they are in a better position to show compassionate empathy. When engaging with our children, model active listening. To help them listen carefully to others, show them how to look for clues in body language which give an insight into what others are feeling. Encourage them to make sure they have understood the viewpoints of others by double checking they have grasped the message.

👍 Give it a Try!

Take every opportunity to teach your child about listening to others to understand what they are feeling.

- Ask them to imagine themselves in the shoes of others.
- How would they feel in that situation?
- Have they ever experienced a similar situation?
- How could they help that person?

Talk to them explicitly about friendship, and the qualities of good friends. Teach them that friendships change and evolve and explain the difference between being popular and having good friendships.

Books can be a wonderful way to teach empathy. When reading stories to young children encourage them to put themselves into the place of the characters, and to think about what they might do in that situation. This can also help our children to see others as equal to themselves. We are all human, and even though the children we see on the news, or hear about in the media, may live far away, they have feelings and emotions, just as we do.

👍 **Give it a Try!**

In approaching the issue of empathy, reframing our children's views helps if they are focusing on a negative in others. Encourage them to look for the good in people, or to consider the challenging behaviour of others with empathy.

If they tell you their friend was in a bad mood this morning, ask them to think about why that might be.

- Could it be that she is worried about something?
- Maybe she didn't sleep well?
- Maybe she had a row with her mum before school?

Remind them also to see the positive qualities of others. If they tell you their friend is always interrupting them, you can agree that yes, he is still struggling to learn how to take turns, but on the other hand he is also very kind if he thinks any of his friends are upset.

From a young age, we can encourage our children to show kindness to others. As a family we can engage in opportunities to volunteer or give back to the community. There are plenty of ways to do this - taking part in a neighbourhood clean-up day; taking part in local charity events; donating unwanted toys; having a cake sale or a lemonade stand for a local charity. There are many ways our children can volunteer. Joining organisations like the Brownies, Girl Guides or Boy Scouts, who coordinate opportunities for volunteering can be worthwhile. Not only is your child gaining new experiences, but they are also developing teamwork skills, learning life skills, and building empathy and social skills. Taking part in activities like this help our children to develop an awareness of the importance of giving back. It develops our children's understanding of other people's challenges, helping them to connect with the reality of others experiencing difficulties. It will also give them a great sense of accomplishment in having helped others.

 It Takes a Village

In her book *Roots and Wings: Childhood Needs a Revolution*[17], Alex Koster cites an excerpt based on Loren Eiseley's story *The Star Thrower* which reminds us of the importance of empathy and small acts of kindness:

A man was walking on the beach one day and noticed a boy who was reaching down, picking up a starfish and throwing it in the ocean.

As he approached, he called out, "Hello! What are you doing?"

The boy looked up and said, "I'm throwing starfish into the ocean."

"Why are you throwing starfish into the ocean?" asked the man.

"The tide stranded them. If I don't throw them in the water before the sun comes up, they'll die," came the answer.

"Surely you realize that there are miles of beach, and thousands of starfish. You'll never throw them all back, there are too many. You can't possibly make a difference."

The boy listened politely, then picked up another starfish. As he threw it back into the sea, he said, "It made a difference for that one."

CHAPTER 5

PARENTING WITH PATIENCE:
PROMOTING POSITIVE BEHAVIOUR

What our children need most, money can't buy.
Our children need human connection.
A healthy, strong parent-child bond, created through consistent, loving
connection, is essential to our children's wellbeing and optimal devel-
opment. This bond is also the key to our effectiveness as parents.
Pam Leo

Parents often cite challenging behaviour as one of the most stressful aspects of parenting. When we feel our children are not co-operating, we sometimes think we need to have greater control over them. But controlling children suggests breaking their spirit, and that is not what we want to do. If we compare the relationship between parent and child to a marriage, we don't use manipulation or threats or bribery within that partnership. In most relationships, other than those with our children, we use connection to make our needs clear. It follows then, that we should use connection when we aim to parent with patience. So why does this not always come naturally to us?

What Kind of Parent am I?

When we look at challenging behaviour, we tend to solely consider the child, but it can be useful to look at our own parenting styles as these strongly influence our responses to, and our connections with, our children. Research has shown how different parenting styles can result in various long-term effects on our children.

 Learning from Psychology

In psychology, parenting behaviour is considered under four different parenting styles[18]. These are authoritarian, permissive, authoritative, and uninvolved. These four styles are based on two dimensions: parental warmth (related to affection) and control (related to promoting respect). The very fact you are reading this book shows you are not an uninvolved parent (indifferent and dismissive of your child and their development), so let's look at the other three styles.

The authoritarian approach takes the "Because I said so" approach to discipline. This parent values obedience and tends to impose their own will on their children, so levels of warmth are lower than levels of control. These children may well conform well to rules and be obedient, however research has linked this parenting style to low self-esteem and anxiety in older children. This approach does not encourage autonomy or independence. If we want our children to obey our demands without question, we are not supporting them to develop an enquiring mind or critical thinking skills.

In contrast, the permissive parenting style is more the "I'm her best friend" approach. Permissive parents believe parents should not impose their will on children but should be available to them as resources. We are looking at high levels of warmth but low levels of control. Although this parenting style focuses very much on nurturing, it can also result in issues as few rules or boundaries are established. In order to create a secure and stable environment for our children, consistency and routine are important. Research has shown these children can struggle with self-regulation and self-control in the long term.

Somewhere in the middle of these two styles is the authoritative parenting style which focuses on warm interactions while parents attempt to shape their children's behaviour with explanation and encouragement. In this case, levels of warmth and control are well balanced. Parents who are authoritative are nurturing, but also set high expectations, so both discussion and independence are encouraged. They set limits and have clearly outlined consequences for specific behaviour. Research has consistently shown that children raised by authoritative parents are more likely to become independent, self-reliant, socially accepted and academically successful.

In all honesty, none of us use just one of these parenting styles. The day could start off where we have slept in, late for school, and our authoritarian style kicks in as we order our children to move more quickly. Perhaps we might make threats about what we might do if they don't move faster! That afternoon we could end up rushing to the supermarket after the school run with three tired and cranky children who are begging for treats. Maybe we are too tired to argue, permissiveness takes over, and we give in to all their requests. Later that evening, as we are putting them to bed and reading them a bedtime story, we become more authoritative and take the time to explain the reasons behind our rules about bedtimes.

We know the way we parent is related to the parenting style we were brought up with. We may think we parent very differently to our own parents, but how often in a moment of stress or pressure have you thought to yourself that you can hear your own mother or father in your response? The parenting styles we lived with throughout our formative years have become embedded within us, and when we are feeling challenged, we often resort back to them. Very often our parents and grandparents raised their children in a time when it was believed children should be seen and not heard. It was expected they obey their elders without question. Times have changed, and although respect and obedience are still heavily valued by most parents today, it is well worth considering the parenting style you fall back on when you are under pressure.

Overall, the parenting style we should aim for is authoritative – using rules and consequences while also validating our children's feelings. Most of us hope to raise well-rounded, emotionally strong children who go on to become responsible adults, and we know this type of parenting is most likely to help us achieve these goals.

Parent-Child Connection

The relationship we have with our child is the most powerful tool we can use to help us to respond to their behaviour. Acknowledging how our children feel, and how we communicate with them is key in this process. When thinking about our children's behaviour, we should look at the way in which we are communicating in general.

 The Science Bit!

Our brains are wired to give greater weight to stimuli which are negative, this is called the negativity bias. You may have heard the saying that our brains are like Velcro for the negative and Teflon for the positive. The idea is that we register negative stimuli more readily than positive and are more likely to dwell on negative events. This is an inbuilt response designed to protect us, so we are more aware of anything in our environment which might expose us to danger. But this bias also applies to our relationships.

Because our brains are strongly weighted towards the negative, we need to have much more positive interactions with our children to balance the scales. Knowing this has led researchers to seek an ideal ratio of positive to negative interactions. Probably the most well-known of these is the work by Psychologist Dr John Gottman who studies adult relationships and recommends a "magic ratio" of 5 to 1 positive to negative interactions between two people for a successful relationship[19]. He argues that every negative interaction at a time of conflict, needs to be counteracted with five positive interactions, and this 5 to 1 ratio provides couples with more stable relationships. Gottman's ratio can be a valuable rule of thumb for parents to consider when looking at our interactions with our children. Rather than considering this ratio as a precise measurement, the key point to remember is to be aware of this balance. In this way, we can try to ensure that the weight of the interactions we have with our children are constructive.

 From the Horse's Mouth

I wonder if we stopped for a moment each day to think about the ratio of every encouraging comment we say to our children, as compared to the negative expressions such as complaints, commands or corrections. What do you think the ratio might be?

Research has shown we are more often issuing a directive or a request for assistance, as compared to accentuating the positive. If you find the negative is outweighing the positive, you can do something about it by focusing more on being encouraging and constructive. Remember, each positive interaction is building the foundations for future communication and connection.

Also think of how, from birth, babies are pre-programmed to seek interactions with their caregivers. Each attempt at communication from the baby, cooing, smiling, or crying, is an opportunity for the parent to engage in what we call a serve and return process. As the parent and child interact with each other, communicating with attention and responding to the contact from each other, connections within the brain of the child are being strengthened.

 Learning from Psychology

In 1975, Edward Tronick and colleagues developed a procedure called the *Still Face Experiment* which studied how babies crave human connection[20]. The experiment involved a mother facing her baby holding a still face, meaning she showed no facial expression for a few minutes, while the reactions of the baby were observed. Usually babies make repeated attempts to engage with the mother, and quickly become agitated if they fail to gain a response. The experiment acts as a reminder of the importance of reciprocal social exchanges between babies and their caregivers. Examination of the brain scans of babies who have been brought up with responsive human connections show many different parts of their brains light up through nurturing parenting. Meanwhile, the scans of babies who have not benefited from these responsive relationships are different, with the amygdala (the area central to the fear response) most lit up, showing these children are most focused on survival than their more securely attached counterparts.

This research reminds us how parenting is a relationship, which is why connection is one of the most important aspects of our interactions with our children. It is valuable on the good days, the days when parenting seems easy, when everyone is getting along, and the family bonds are strong. We often think these are the days in which we more easily build connections with our children, the happy moments. But it is also important on the days when tempers are frayed, and patience can seem hard to find. Bear in mind, connection is the glue which binds us as a family and these bonds help us to find breathing space during difficult times. Connection is the boat which keeps us all afloat. Most of us would agree when we feel connected to our child our relationship is stronger, and it is easier to face challenges. This results in trust within a relationship, and when a child feels connected to their parent it is easier to communicate with each other.

Connection is also built during moments when we share vulnerability. There are times, perhaps at the early stage of a new friendship, when someone shares their vulnerability, and in that instant, everything changes within the relationship. Those moments when someone shares with us their fears, insecurities, or worries, are often moments when our connection with them deepens, and the relationship is stronger as a result. This is when we really listen to each other without judgement.

The same applies with our children. Connection is strengthened when we take the time to listen to their innermost feelings and provide an empathetic and supportive ear. There are endless opportunities during the day for us to find moments of connection with our child. They include those everyday moments when we sit and spend time with them, when we listen to what they have to say, when we pause and take a moment to share an experience with them. The first moments when they wake and those final moments before they go to bed at night are just as important.

It is when we lose connection with our children that they are likely to show us through their behaviour that all is not well. We have all heard the saying that love is spelled T-I-M-E. Oh how true this is!

Although parenting can be stressful and frustrating when we are faced with challenging behaviour, taking time to connect with each child can make all the difference. We want our children to feel loved and listened to.

Pam Leo, author of *Connection Parenting, Parenting Through Connection Instead of Coercion*, and founder of the *Connection Parenting*™ workshop series, reminds us of the value of such connection. She uses the analogy of filling a child's love cup, which she tells us is as important as meeting their physical need for food. Spending this time with them, with one-on-one attention, eye contact, physical touch, laughter, and play, is exactly the emotional fuel our children need. Leo advises "Either we spend the time meeting children's emotional needs by filling their cup with love, or we spend time dealing with the behaviours caused by the unmet needs. Either way we spend the time."

This connection is important throughout our parenting journey. On those difficult parenting days when we need to call on all our strength, these are the days when strong connections make life easier to manage. Children who feel connected to us are happier, more loving, and more cooperative.

👍 **Give it a Try!**

Leo recommends having special one-on-one time with your child every day as a way of developing strong parent-child connection[21]. The aim is that children spend this time consistently and individually with the parent strengthening their bond. She also reminds us of the importance of embedding play during this time. Her argument is that if we can re-discover the joy of play, it helps us to understand and respond to the needs of our children. She reminds us that actively playing with children is the most powerful way to fill their love cup. The most important thing to remember during this time is that 100% attention is important, meaning no engaging with our phones!

She acknowledges that for many of us, being playful no longer comes naturally as adults. But she reassures us that engaging in roughhousing, silliness, and the active play of chase and capture, is exactly what our children need. She promises us that the giggles and laughter, the affection and connection that build during this type of play are well worth taking a leap of faith for!

The idea of spending 15 minutes each day attuned to our children is an idea most of us can get on board with.

Why Does Challenging Behaviour Occur?

We sometimes say that our young children are experts at testing our patience. Most parents would say they have crumbled under pressure at some point when they feel their child is pushing their buttons. In fact, testing our limits is developmentally appropriate for younger children and is part of the learning process as they make sense of their world. Try not to take it personally! Young children desperately want to assert their independence, but their impulse control and self-regulation are not well developed. So, when they feel stressed or frustrated, impulsive behaviours intensify.

We sometimes think we should discipline our children by punishing them, but the word discipline does not mean to punish. In fact, it means to teach, guide, and instruct.

We often hear children's behaviour described as the tip of the iceberg. In order to understand it, we need to look beneath the surface. The behaviour is visible on the surface, and it provides clues to what is happening underneath which is where the root causes can be found. These are the emotions and needs they struggle to fully explain because they don't have the words or understanding. When the child's needs are being met, this will show on the surface. Equally, when the child's needs are not being met, this is reflected in their behaviour. Viewing behaviour in this way changes our perspective. We see the behaviour as a form of communication.

 From the Horse's Mouth

When my children were young and I was faced with challenging behaviour, I found I would always focus on what I could do to change the behaviour. In effect, get rid of it. As my children grew older I realised I should be asking myself, what does the behaviour tell me about my child? So, now I try to focus on understanding *why* my child might be struggling, rather than trying to control them. Trying to remember this difference has helped me to approach challenging behaviour in a more calm and positive way.

Sometimes challenging behaviour occurs because of how we relate to the child. When our children are frustrated with life, how we communicate with them can either increase or decrease the behaviour. One thing which can really escalate challenging behaviour is shouting. Shouting at a child only serves to heighten your stress levels and show the child that shouting is a way of communicating. It is the equivalent of an adult tantrum. You are role modelling the very behaviour you are trying to discourage in the child.

Toddlers and Preschoolers

Children of this age run very much on what we call the emotional brain rather than the thinking brain which is not as well developed at this age.

 The Science Bit!

An example used to demonstrate this (and no, I would not recommend trying this, as it will deliberately provoke your child!) is called the *Broken Biscuit Experiment*[22]. In this experiment, two four-year old's sitting together are given a biscuit each. One child is given a whole biscuit, while the other child is given a biscuit that has been broken into two halves. The child given the broken biscuit is likely to have a strong emotional reaction because their feeling brain responds immediately with how the other child was given the perfect biscuit and they were given the 'damaged' biscuit. As adults we recognise (because we are using our thinking brains) that there is no real difference between the two biscuits – two halves make a whole – but the child can only see the world in an emotional way, and that is how they respond.

Knowing brain development plays a part in their responses can help us to understand, and hopefully react, in a calmer manner. One of the joys of the way children this age respond is the absolute honesty they show in their emotions. They shower us with love and affection when they feel it. If they are happy, we see big smiles and laughter. They are equally as honest when they feel anger, frustration, jealousy, or fear. During these years, the aim is to learn to identify their emotions and how to respond to them.

Developmentally little ones are programmed to assert their independence. Rather than thinking of the terrible twos or terrible threes, if we remember they are learning to be more independent it can help us to parent more calmly when they are testing the boundaries.

One of the main issues parents report in the toddler and preschool years are emotional outbursts, or tantrums. These are usually caused by frustration, lack of language to express feelings, or the need for autonomy, and often follow frustration which has been building over time.

During these years, children are rapidly acquiring language, however, toddlers generally understand more than they can express. They might know what they want to say, but emotion is swirling around inside them, and they simply do not have the words to express those feelings. The good news is, as language skills improve, tantrums tend to decrease. But how do we help them navigate some of these more difficult emotions?

Navigating Emotions

Having the words to express how they are feeling is an important place to begin when understanding our emotions. In your everyday conversations with your child, give them the words to express how they are feeling, for example, "You seem very happy to see Granny today," or "I'm guessing you feel sad because Bobby can't come to play?" Instead of telling them how they feel - because we don't really know for sure - guess at what they might be feeling. In this way we are letting them know we are trying to understand their emotions. We are helping them consider and name their emotions.

💡 Top Tip!

You can also tell them about how you deal with your own feelings. "I was feeling so frustrated this morning when I dropped the cup on the floor. I had to take five deep breaths to help me feel calm again." Children need to know all feelings are OK, and it is normal to experience anger or sadness if they are having a difficult experience.

Most young children understand emotions such as happy and sad but may not have the labels or definitions for the range of emotions in between. Naming the full array of emotions will help them make finer discriminations between feelings. To say, "That must be so frustrating for you" or "I'm guessing you feel cross your little sister did that," or "You look a little worried about this," gives them a larger pool of words to use when describing how they feel. Learning to name and recognise their own emotions will also help them to understand the emotions of others.

Stories are another great way to talk to children about emotions, and to help them in naming their emotions. When reading to them, ask them how they think the characters are feeling. Have they ever felt that way? What could they do if they feel that way again? Give them some ideas and strategies to use.

- Maybe they could ask you for a hug when they are feeling scared?
- Maybe they can get their blankie and sit in a quiet place if they are feeling tired?
- Maybe they could use their words to tell you how they are feeling?

Use quiet, calm times to support them in talking about their feelings and practice the strategies they would like to try. For example, "Everyone feels angry at times. I know you get angry when your big brother will not play with you, but it's not OK to hit him. Instead you can take some deep breaths then tell him how you feel."

 Top Tip!

Give them plenty of time to practice these strategies, and lots of praise when they put them into place.

Toddlers desperately want a sense of control over their lives. This creates the perfect condition for power struggles as the child *absolutely* believes they can do the task themselves, or *absolutely* believes they need to have whatever they see at that moment. When your son stands at the top of the stairs in his Buzz Lightyear suit, and shouts, "To Infinity and Beyond," he is absolutely sure he can leap with confidence down those stairs. When you intervene telling him to be careful, not to leap from the top but to start slowly by leaping from the second step up, the stage is set for a tantrum. At this age, it is difficult to accept that you can't do everything you want (and firmly have the confidence to attempt!) and to accept you can't have everything your heart desires. Frustration is unavoidable as these little ones learn how the world works. It is part and parcel of the learning experience at this age. Being able to look at this behaviour as being age appropriate, and developmentally sound, will remind you your son is not bad, he is simply a preschooler! When they are caught up in their emotion and are struggling with anger or frustration, it is important they know we can see this is hard for them, and we can sit it out and wait with them until things get better. We will stay with them and wait even when they are filled with all this emotion.

👍 Give it a Try!

We can take steps to avoid strong emotional outbursts.

- First of all, choose your battles! If you expect a little one to follow lots of rules, they are likely to struggle. Instead try to give children control over little things in their world.

- It is also important to know your child's limits, say in terms of hunger or tiredness. Expecting them to behave well when they are tired after a long day can be unrealistic. When possible try to manage your expectations of them when they are tired and hungry.

- Considering the environment can also be an issue. If I know taking my child through the toy section of my local supermarket without letting her stop and look at the toys is likely to cause her frustration, then it makes sense to avoid that section.

- Children this age live in the moment. It can help to keep certain, off-limits items out of sight in our homes. If you don't want the youngest child using his older sibling's markers, then keep them out of his sight. Try to keep the more age appropriate materials within reach.

If you see a tantrum brewing, showing empathy is the best approach. Calmly let them know you can see they are struggling with their emotions. Saying something like, "I'm guessing it's hard when your brothers have to go to training and can't stay home to play," shows them you are aware of the feelings they are experiencing. You are trying to diffuse the situation in advance.

Distraction and re-direction also work well when you see a situation has potential to cause a tantrum. Distraction can work particularly well when it involves something unexpected. Even saying something such as, "Wow, is that a little robin out in the garden? Let's have a look," can completely distract them from the original issue. Re-direction towards something exciting can also help, for example the suggestion they put on their wellies and go for a splash in a puddle outside can completely distract a toddler from potential upset.

Calming Tantrums

When tantrums happen (and they will happen!) the most important thing you can do is stay calm yourself. Take a few deep breaths and understand the cause. If you meet the tantrum with compassion rather than anger, it helps. Remember sometimes little things (getting the red cup rather than the yellow one!) are important to the child at that moment in time. What seems silly to you is significant to them. The key again is to empathise.

 Top Tip!

This is not the moment to teach your child an important life lesson! Instead you want to connect with her. Empathising is not rewarding the tantrum; it is recognising how the child is struggling and acknowledging that you are attempting to meet their need for connection and understanding.

When I say connect, I don't mean to have a conversation! They are awash with adrenaline during a tantrum, so the best response is to say nothing and simply stay present as a calming influence. When they are calming down, acknowledge how upset the child is. Recognise how they are feeling, rather than explaining why they cannot have what they wanted. Calmly showing compassion and empathy when a child is struggling with these big feelings can help them to dissipate.

If you are in a public place, again take a few deep breaths and respond calmly. Try not to let the disapproval of others affect you. I know it is difficult, but if you block out and ignore any disapproving glances, it helps you to focus on what is really important – your child.

 It Takes a Village

My son had a very public meltdown yesterday in the supermarket. I sat on the floor with him... hugging him when he let me. The amount of people who shook their heads at us, and made comments about showing him who is the boss floored me... I think it's very hard for a parent (particularly a first-time parent like me) who chooses to show empathy during these meltdowns and big feelings, because our society is not conducive to that method of parenting. People view it as being a 'push over' or 'being walked over' instead of taking it at face value – a child who is in desperate need of connection and comfort. I will continue to listen to the little voice within telling me to love him through those feelings but I can see why it can be difficult for parents to drown out the 'noise' of society and their judgements in those situations.

[Credit: Sara White via Facebook]

I love Sara's insight, and the confidence she has in listening to her own inner voice, rather than bowing to the disapproval of others.

Once the tantrum has ended, it is important to reconnect. Don't insist they talk about their emotions. They probably can't explain why they were so upset. Instead, reassure them that everyone needs to cry sometimes and that you love them no matter what. When the child has calmed down, praise her for regaining control, offer a hug, and let her know you are proud of her for getting through it.

Issues with Sharing

Learning to share things is another big issue for this age group. They are often passionate about wanting one exact thing, and no other thing will do. In fact, the word *mine* can be one of their favourite words! One of the issues with sharing at this age is that the child hasn't developed the ability to see things from another child's perspective yet. They are still very egocentric (focused on their own thoughts and needs) and they struggle with impulse control. It seems, as adults, we expect quite a lot from them at this age.

 What Does the Research Say?

Research from the UK found 70% of parents thought a child should be able to share by three years old, while more than half believed children should have enough impulse control to resist the desire to do something forbidden by age three. In reality, we know these skills are only developing at that age. Understanding our children haven't developed these abilities yet can help us manage our expectations and our frustration when we see children struggle with sharing.

If we are honest with ourselves, often when we ask our little ones to share, we are really asking them to give what they have to another child. This is certainly how it looks from their perspective! You may find as they are learning to share, they will engage in selective sharing. They may share with a friend on a playdate more easily than with a younger sibling. Or they may share most of their toys with a friend but will also hide their favourite possessions away when the same friend comes to visit. They are learning to share by doing so in the least threatening circumstances.

It is worth remembering that when a child wants to keep a toy they are playing with, it can be a sign that they are engrossed in the activity. It is in those moments when a child is fully immersed in play that the most significant learning takes place. In these circumstances it is not helpful to expect the child to share. Instead, we can use it as an opportunity to encourage turn-taking. If a child is in the middle of their play, it is more effective to teach them to say, "I am still playing with this, but you can have your turn when I am finished." In this way, we are moving from the concept of sharing to teach them about turn-taking instead. You are also helping your child to communicate their needs to their friends.

If a row breaks out over a toy, avoid immediately rushing in to intervene. Give a little breathing space to see if the children can work it out themselves. If they are struggling, using a timer to control turns can help children to learn about turn-taking. But if sharing is an ongoing challenge, the child waiting their turn might need a little bit of adult support while they are waiting. Saying something like, "Can you show me how this toy works while you are waiting?" can make all the difference. They know you are there with them sharing the time while they wait

– sharing their pain if you like! But remember, learning to share is a long process, and it is not something which comes easily to young children. I think we all know some adults who still struggle with it!

 Top Tip!

Even though this time can be challenging for parents, remember they love you unconditionally, and even though none of us can keep our patience all the time, the more we model a calm response, the more they learn to behave in the same way.

School Age Children

As children start primary school, they are beginning to understand the relationship between actions and consequences. Consistency is key here. Decide on the rules which are important to you (not too many!) and uphold them. Once again, pick those battles. What is important to one parent, is not to another. Don't worry about what your sister, or your friend, or your mother-in-law thinks is important. Decide what aspects of your child's behaviour are important to you and focus on those aspects. And don't sweat the small stuff! If you adjust what you can reasonably accommodate, it will save the battles for the things which are non-negotiable. Maybe for you it could be bedtime, or healthy eating. It is whatever matters most to you personally. Explain your rules and why they are important, instead of the "because I said so" approach. Be specific about why you need them to do something. Let them know what you expect in advance and be clear about what constitutes good behaviour. It can be helpful to get the child to repeat the request back to you, to check they understand.

From the Horse's Mouth

Start from a positive perspective. Catch them being good and praise them when they do well. One method which a friend told me about when my children were younger, is called *The Rubber Band Method*. You put five hair bobbins on your left wrist. When you catch them being good during the day, tell them, and move one of the bands over to your right wrist. Aim to move all five over each day.

Our language and the way we communicate is also important. Ask yourself are you using the *You* message, or the *I* message. Often when we are frustrated at our children's behaviour we tend to use *You*. Saying things such as, "You never listen to me," or "You're not doing that the right way." The *You* message feels like a finger being pointed when you are on the receiving end of it. It makes the child feel they are the problem. A much more effective approach is the *I* message. Here I am focusing on what I need from the child, by letting them know my needs, or how I feel. For example, by saying something like, "Michael, I want to start making the dinner. I really need you to empty the dishwasher so I can start," or "Kira, I want to make sure we have time to get out to the park, so I need you to help me finish tidying up." It shifts the perspective from one of blame, to one where I am asking the child to support my needs. Children are compassionate by nature, so engaging their compassion by connecting, rather than making threats, can be an effective way to positively manage behaviour.

Top Tip!

Another useful approach for when a child is digging in their heels and doesn't want to do what you ask is the, "When we...then we can..." approach. To you, it may be obvious why your child needs to undertake a task, but to her, not so much! If your child is refusing to do what they are asked, do your best not to get caught up in a battle of wills. Instead, work with them, stay calm and use the phrase, "When we...then we can..." For example, "When we put on our wellies, then we can go to the park," or "When we finish lunch, then we can take the dog for a walk."

If the child breaks one of your non-negotiable rules, explain exactly what she is doing that is unacceptable. Saying, "Don't do that," will not be effective as the child may have no idea of what exactly she has done wrong! Explain both the right thing to do, as well as the wrong thing. Blaming or shaming children can make them feel worse about themselves and will not diffuse a situation. A situation where a child's behaviour is unacceptable to you is also an opportunity to teach them how to express their feelings and emotions in a positive way.

We want our children to know it is ok to feel angry. What is not ok is hitting their little sister as a result of that anger. We criticise the behaviour, not the child. Bring yourself to the child's level and make direct eye contact. In this way, the child will see you are speaking to him (albeit in a calm and considered way) and that you mean what you are saying. Very often when a child is distressed our instinct is to fix things. We try to control the emotion and make it go away. But we can't wave a magic wand and vanish away a child's unhappy feelings. What we can do is help them learn how to manage what they do about them.

> 👍 **Give it a Try!**
>
> The first thing is to acknowledge the feelings. We allow them to experience the feeling, rather than immediately jump in and try to solve the problem. We want to emphasise our presence, and a sense of connection.
>
> Then we encourage them to speak about their feelings. When children are angry or frustrated, they are at the height of their emotions and it can be quite frightening for them. Having someone name that feeling and acknowledge it, can be comforting for a child who is having difficulty verbalising what they are feeling.
>
> It is important to separate who they are from what they do, so the message is, "I love you, but I don't love what you're doing."

Regulating Emotions

Various psychologists have examined the concepts of *Top Down* and *Bottom Up* behaviour when considering our children's brain development in terms of self-regulation[23]. They suggest that children who can't seem to behave themselves are in fact unable to perform at the level we expect of them. Top Down behaviour is controlled, intentional and planned. In other words, the child decides what to do and does it. Bottom Up behaviour is reflexive, automatic or a stress response. It is not a conscious decision but happens when the child is feeling threatened.

When dealing with challenging behaviour we need to consider whether we are witnessing Top Down or Bottom Up behaviour. Based on the concept of Neuroception (the child's subconscious monitoring of threat and safety) it is argued that the child who does not feel safe, is not capable of self-regulation. Each child is an individual and it takes specific connections to support them. For some of our children with overly sensitive nervous systems it is difficult to behave in a Top Down way. We expect the child to listen to reason, and to change their behaviour in a logical way, but their brain is in a state of stress and they can't respond to reason. Stress is suggested to be one of the major contributors in difficulty with self-regulation and this reminds us to be compassionate when supporting children with challenging behaviour.

 Learning From Psychology

To connect with children when in a stressed state, Dr Bruce Perry of the *Child Trauma Academy* suggests we use the three R's: Regulate, Relate, and Reason.

- To regulate means to offer soothing comfort so the child can regulate their stress response. This can be done by calmly offering a reassuring presence. Even if they are being difficult, or using a disrespectful tone of voice, we need to not respond in kind. Instead, we should remain calm and soothe them, just as you would if they were physically hurt and lashing out. This helps bring them out of their reactive state.

- To relate means to connect to the child by offering an empathetic response. Saying something like, "That must be very hard for you," or "It looks like you are having a hard time." This helps the child to move to a more receptive place where they can engage with us.

- To reason means to engage with the child's thinking brain, but this can only be done after the other two stages. We could say something like, "How can I help?" This is the time when they are in a more receptive state of mind and we can reason and discuss their behaviour with them, and how they might better respond in future.

For many of us, our first response is to jump immediately towards explanation and rationale, when the child is not in a state where they can engage on that level. Calm reassurance and empathy need to always come first.

Once again we are reminded of the adult-child connection. In order to truly connect with our child, we need to remain calm in the face of their challenging behaviour. Slowing down, and being present with our children, creates the time to connect with them. This is not only important at the point of misbehaviour, but greater connection on a daily basis will help the child to self-regulate.

The wonderful L.R. Knost[24] sums it all up when she reminds us to respond to our children with L.O.V.E. She says:

> Respond to your
> children with love in
> their worst moments
> their broken moments
> their angry moments
> their selfish moments
> their lonely moments
> their frustrated moments
> their inconvenient moments
> because it is in their most
> unlovable human moments
> that they most need to feel loved.

Instead of responding to our child in haste, she advises that so many problems can be avoided when we respond with L.O.V.E. She asks us to think of L.O.V.E. as Listen, Observe, Validate and Empathise.

Connecting with our children starts with really listening to what the child is trying to tell us. Then be present and supportive, watching to see when they are calm enough to engage with us. The focus is on soothing. We want the child to know we are calm, and that they are safe.

You are one of the most important people in your child's life. Your validation is important to them. Giving your child your time and attention is one way to validate, by acknowledging their feelings, their emotions, and letting them know you value and respect them.

What does it mean to validate your child's feelings?
It means to let them know they are understood and
that their feelings are felt by you. Remember it's all
about connection!

We can focus on connection through our words and our tone of voice. When we say, "I know it is hard when we have to leave the playground, and I'm guessing it makes you feel sad," it shows our child that they are seen and heard when they are struggling. Showing empathy in this way can support the child as they learn to self-regulate. They are looking to us for support and guidance. If we can handle our own frustration and show patience when they are struggling, we are modelling self-control.

Only after connection should we move on to reasoning. Once you have supported your child in regulating their emotion, you can then move on to discuss the limits you have set and why you have set them. This response works just as well with teens as with younger children.

👍 Give it a Try!

- The core of these approaches is to see discipline as teaching and to view it as an opportunity to guide our children in how to deal with their emotions.
- In order to teach a child who has lost control, we need to get them back into a receptive state rather than a reactive one.
- Connection and showing empathy are always underpinning this message.

- The key is to remember our children have poorly developed impulse control and are designed to test boundaries.
- Instead of punishment we want to have calm discussions when we are connected to the child, supporting them to engage with our rules and boundaries.
- The aim is that as our children get older they will have learned to self-discipline and to manage their emotions, so that they will understand what is expected of them in the adult world.
- Remember, connection should come before correction.

Expressing and Managing Anger

During the early years our children are slowly becoming more skilled at self-regulation. If we think about a 7-year-old expressing their anger as opposed to a 3-year-old, the older child will be better able to handle situations and emotions due to developmental maturity. Equally a teenager should be better able to manage their emotions more than a younger child. We play an important role in supporting our children in expressing their anger. To enable our children to express their emotions well, it helps to provide them with some strategies to use at times of anger or frustration.

I mentioned earlier about the importance of naming emotions to increase a child's emotional literacy. In order to get children to focus on what they are feeling, it can also be useful to have them think about how their body responds to stress and try to locate the feeling in the body. To do this, ask them to think about how their body reacts to anger: for example, butterflies in their tummy, racing heart and fast breathing. They are recognising that it is the emotion which is bringing about this feeling in their body. Every child has moments when their emotions control their actions, but we can help our children to acknowledge and respond to their feelings rather than suppress them. When they are calm, we can develop strategies for them to use when they are faced with difficult feelings. The mindfulness activities we will cover in the next chapter are equally as useful for anger management as they are for anxiety. However, there are strategies your child can use when faced with overwhelming emotions.

👍 Give it a Try!

Here are some possible strategies your child can put into place to help express and manage their anger:
- Count up to, or down from, 10.
- Tell someone how you are feeling.
- Take 5 deep breaths.
- Run, skip, or jump.
- Draw what you are feeling.
- Put the palms of your hands together, press then release, three times.
- Go to a calm spot to cool down.
- Squeeze a stress ball.
- Do 10 jumping jacks.
- Use positive self-talk, "I can do this," or "let it go."
- Pop bubble wrap.
- Sing your favourite song out loud.
- Write down what makes you feel angry then rip up the paper.

Reviewing this list with your child can give them some ideas for how to cope with their frustration while they learn to regulate their emotions. Getting outside as much as possible with our children when we are feeling challenged can also help everyone in the house to work off their frustration.

Parents Keeping Calm

One of the most difficult things to do as a parent is to remain calm and kind when faced with challenging behaviour, but we know that when children are treated with respect and kindness, they learn to treat others the same way. Finding calmer and more positive ways to respond, and trying to react in a more consistent way, can help us to parent well when under pressure. But we are less able to deal with our children's challenging behaviour when we are tired, over-worked, or stressed ourselves. It is important to take care of ourselves so we can take care of our children. The old saying about putting on our own oxygen mask before helping others is absolutely true. Our child's ability to stay calm is often dependent on our own ability to stay calm. If you are at the end of your tether, it is unlikely you will be able to do that.

Knowing we should stay calm is a different thing to actually being able to do it! Just as we should consider the list of techniques above with our children, it can be important to put in place some coping strategies for ourselves. Walking away, taking a few deep breaths, leaving the room to wash your hands or face to help you calm down, whatever works for you. It is also important to show our children that anger can be channelled in a positive way. Think of ways you can do this, whether it is going for a run, or joining your child on the trampoline to release the energy from the anger. The controlled breathing technique we will cover in the next chapter works just as well for adults as it does for children and is a useful technique for parents to use when we need to calm.

Dealing with challenging behaviour with patience does not come easily to most of us. There is a misconception that parenting by taking a peaceful approach means taking the easy way out. But addressing difficult behaviour respectfully, rather than punitively, can be very demanding and can most definitely test our patience! Sometimes just knowing this, or being aware of the situations that trigger us, can help.

If you do end up losing your temper, remember we are all human. We all get it wrong sometimes. Just as we recognise our children are not perfect, we must allow ourselves the same grace.

Although ongoing physical discipline has been shown to have a negative impact on our children, all of us lose our cool at times, and these one-off moments are very repairable. Our children are learning from us on the days when we get it wrong. We are teaching them that all emotions are valid, none of us are happy all the time, we all have bad days. As parents we are not perfect either. We are human.

At times like this you can give your child a valuable lesson in how you respond to your mistakes. Come back to them when you are calm to repair. By doing so we are teaching them that we all make mistakes, but we can mend as much as possible afterwards. Even after a small conflict or misunderstanding, try saying something like, "I really am sorry I shouted at you. I lost my temper, and that must have been very hard for you. I should have talked calmly, and not shouted in that way. I love you and will try to do better in future." If they see us model contrition, they will do the same. Repairing after conflict also teaches our child that trust, and connection can be restored. They learn about empathy and forgiveness. You are showing them what repair looks and feels like.

But remember saying sorry is only authentic if we follow it up by a change in habits. Thinking about how we might change our behaviour and find new ways to deal with our own anger can help. Every parent needs to develop a toolkit they can use for self-regulation, some strategies we can fall back on when we need to re-balance our emotions. We also need to consider how to look after our own wellbeing as part of this toolkit.

Self-Care

We have all heard the saying, "You can't pour from an empty cup." To be a calm and empathetic parent, you need to show yourself some self-compassion. So many of us dedicate our lives to our children while neglecting our own needs. If we have a bad day, where we lose our cool with our children, it is often a message that we need to take a little time out ourselves. Self-care is restorative, but it usually comes very low on our list of priorities. Think about what you can do to ensure you get some time to yourself, time to recharge your batteries, and a little bit of space to clear your head. Taking this time for yourself on a regular basis will give you the strength to be a better parent.

When considering self-care, it is also important to become aware of our own stress levels. What are your personal triggers? How do you recognise when your patience is wearing thin? It can help to recognise your own stressors and be aware when your energy stores are running low by focusing on the need to recharge. If you are feeling that you don't have a second to spare to devote to yourself, that is a warning sign that self-care is needed. If you can take a little time to fill your own cup, you will have more patience and energy to support your family. While there are many different self-care strategies, it is worth taking a moment to work out which might work best for you. Feeling better will help you to be the best parent you can be.

It Takes a Village

I asked a group of parents what strategies they use when they need some space. Have a look at the list below for some ideas for self-care. Make your own list of suggestions which resonate with you and commit to undertaking one activity on your list every day.

- phone a friend for a quick chat
- get out for a walk, preferably in nature
- give yourself permission to stop multi-tasking
- take a 5-minute coffee or hot chocolate break
- ask a friend or family member to babysit
- listen to some uplifting music
- limit your 'to do list' to a 5-task maximum each day
- light a scented candle
- have a digital detox for the evening
- walk the dog
- schedule some catch-up time with a friend
- download a self-care app like Headspace or Calm
- focus on taking long deep breaths for five minutes
- take a shower or bath with relaxing music playing
- write down three things you are grateful for every day
- go to bed a half hour earlier tonight

Taking the time to engage in one small act which will nourish your soul, one small act of self-compassion, will help to replenish your energy and patience.

Finally, if you find yourself consistently angry, seek some support. Talk to a friend or family member, speak to your GP or a counsellor. There are an array of parenting supports available, many of which are free resources, and which can provide very concrete skills in positive behaviour management. When we are calm and more confident in our parenting it results in a happier household.

CHAPTER 6

ANXIOUS CHILDREN IN AN ANXIOUS WORLD

We would like to think of history as progress,
but if progress is measured by the mental health and happiness of
young people, then we've been going backward at least since the
early 1950s.

Prof Peter Gray

Irish Children's Mental Health

The emotional wellbeing of our children is as important as their physical health, and child mental health is a growing concern for Irish parents. By the age of thirteen, 1 in 3 children in Ireland will have experienced some form of mental health difficulty.

> *To put this in perspective, for any family with three children, it is likely one will have some mental health issue before they are a teenager.*

This figure is higher than their counterparts in the UK or the US, and by the time they are 24, half of them struggle. In terms of the most common issues, anxiety is high on the list[26].

What does the Research Say?

The *My World 2 Survey* on mental health in Ireland involved more than 19,000 twelve to twenty-five-year olds[27]. This was a follow up to a 2012 study and found significant increases in levels of anxiety and depression since that date. 22% of teens (12-19 years) and 26% of young adults (18-25 years) reported severe anxiety. The study found a significant relationship between time spent online (more than three hours a day) and higher levels of anxiety and depression. Having said that, we don't fully understand whether this time spent online is causing anxiety in our children. It is equally possible our more anxious children are spending long hours online which in turn increases anxiety.

From a positive perspective, the *My World 2 Survey* reinforced something we already understand from attachment theory. The presence of a consistently supportive adult figure was noted as one of the most important factors at times of distress. For those of us with a child who struggles with anxiety this is an important point to remember. As we increase our knowledge and understanding of what is happening to our children in the spiral of anxiety, it leaves us in a stronger place to support them.

What is Anxiety?

If we are to fully support our children, it is important we understand what they are experiencing when they feel anxious. Let's start by considering what anxiety is, and the science behind what is happening to our children when they experience it.

Anxiety is a state of apprehension which develops when we anticipate a threatening situation, whether that situation is real or imagined. It is our internal protection mechanism, our inner alarm, which helps us to survive danger. It is perfectly normal, and we all experience it from time to time.

There are three interlinked aspects to anxiety: our thoughts (what we say to ourselves) which lead to physical feelings (how our body responds) and our behaviours (our actions).

If a child is worried about their mum not collecting them from school, this can cause a pain in their tummy or their heart to race. This then makes them want to avoid going to school. Seeing the connection between thoughts, feelings and our behaviours can help children better understand anxiety.

Anxiety impacts on our children's lives in various ways. Children who struggle with anxiety might be fearful of making mistakes, or of making a fool of themselves in public. They might avoid sports or performance related activities, where they feel they will be on show. They are often overly aware of the judgements of others. They can struggle to fall asleep at night, as they lie in bed ruminating over the day's events. Although we all reflect to some extent, these children tend to go around in circles which can become problematic. Some will have difficulty sleeping alone. They may wake in the middle of the night and want to sneak into their parent's bed. They could be the sort of child who is due to go to a sleepover, but instead of having that glass of wine, you wait, half expecting a 2am phone call to say they want you to come and bring them home.

From the Horse's Mouth

The issue of sleeping alone in their bed can be a difficult one! All three of my children would sneak into our bed at night when they were young. Even for adults, everything can look more frightening when you wake in the middle of the night. I could always understand why a child, anxious or not, might need the reassurance of a parent's touch when the world seems a scary place. I remember a friend telling me that her little girl once asked why her mum and dad were allowed share a bed, when she, who got scared more easily, had to sleep alone! My friend struggled to answer the question, and I have to admit, it stopped me in my tracks too.

In the school context, there are various ways anxiety can present. Some children are listening to every word from the teacher, anxiously working on what they have been instructed to do, trying to achieve perfection. This is the child who will keep rubbing out their work, worried it is never good enough. Or you can have the child who is not hearing a word the teacher says. As the teacher is talking, they might be thinking about an experience in the yard earlier at break time, worried that their friend was playing with someone else, and asking themselves a million questions about what it could mean. As well as ruminating, they are catastrophising about the situation, anticipating all the possible negative developments which may occur. Anxiety can also result in problems going to school, with the child citing sick tummy, headaches and so on.

One thing is for sure, and it relates to all children,
is that ongoing anxiety disempowers our children.
Something which can help them claw back their power

is having an understanding of what is happening within their bodies. So, it is important to explain anxiety to your child in an age appropriate way.

The first thing is to make clear that anxiety is a good thing. It stems from a system designed to protect us. This can be hard for your child to believe, because anxiety certainly doesn't feel good, but it is important to explain this to them. It is also perfectly natural to feel anxious. For example, when starting a new school year, when performing in the Christmas play, or maybe before a test. But if anxiety starts to flood our systems then it becomes problematic. It is important to understand what is taking place, and to learn about ways to help calm ourselves down to manage our own wellbeing.

Fight or Flight

The Amygdala aka The Toddler

Within our brains, the limbic system helps us to deal with our emotions and our memories. One important part of this system is called the *Amygdala*. The amygdala takes in information from our senses and helps to protect us from any threats in our environment. It reacts quickly when it senses any danger and is like a little internal warrior trying to protect us.

 Top Tip!

I suggest children imagine the amygdala as a little toddler who is trying to protect you. Imagine him right in the centre of your brain, sitting there on guard, ready to respond to any danger. But, if they have any younger siblings who are toddlers, they will know that toddlers don't respond calmly to danger!

When the amygdala receives information from our senses which could mean danger, it instantly starts a reaction inside our bodies to protect us. We call this the fight or flight response. The amygdala thinks something might hurt you, so it springs into action to protect you. This response has helped humans to survive since hunter-gatherer times.

 The Science Bit!

Imagine you are living back in hunter-gatherer times. You are out hunting and hear a rustle in the bushes behind you. Before you can even turn your head to see if there is danger lurking, your amygdala will have responded. It sends out signals to release stress hormones such as adrenaline and cortisol which cause physical reactions inside your body. Your heart pounds, beating faster as blood rushes to your extremities - your arms and hands in case you need to fight, and your legs and feet in case you need to run. Your breathing changes, becoming faster, making you breathless, and you can feel flushed or dizzy. The amygdala sees no need to digest food, as it wants to save energy to fight or flight, so it slows down the digestive system. These responses are all designed to help protect you. The amygdala is preparing you in case you need to either fight a tiger lurking in those bushes or run away from it.

This system helps us to respond to the many challenges we face. But if this response is invoked by everyday life events, then trouble starts.

In our modern world, the amygdala responds to perceived threats which may not need this response. For our children, the amygdala might respond in this way to seeing your friends standing away from you in the school yard whispering to each other. It could respond this way if we do something embarrassing and other students in the class laugh. For older children it could respond this way if we put a photo up on Instagram which gets very few likes. Our worrying thoughts are bringing about the same response as a tiger in the bushes did for our ancestors. The problem is that the amygdala has lightning fast reflexes. It moves to protect us without sending messages to the part of our brain which considers the level of risk and how to respond.

The Prefrontal Cortex aka the Teacher

While the amygdala responds to save our lives, another part of our brain considers if this response is needed in this individual situation. The part of the brain that is responsible for this type of thinking is called the *Prefrontal Cortex*. It is at the front of our brain, in behind our forehead. This is the part of the brain responsible for higher-level thinking – things like organisation, planning, decision making and reasoning. It is the centre of rational, logical thought. This area of the brain helps us work things out, but when we are angry, stressed, or anxious, the amygdala stops information getting to it.

💡 Top Tip!

If your child is imagining the amygdala as a little toddler sitting in the centre of the brain ready for action, then they could imagine the prefrontal cortex as a little teacher, ready to approach a situation with logic.

When a difficult situation arises, the little toddler can take control, and this thinking part of the brain - the little teacher - is turned offline. We are relying on action rather than thought to deal with the situation. This was the perfect response back in hunter-gatherer times when we were out dealing with physically risky situations every day. But it is as if our brains have not caught up in evolutionary terms with our modern world and the challenges it brings us. This very quick response, firing on all cylinders, when we no longer have a physical challenge to respond to, is not always helpful. It can leave us dealing with the fight or flight response and the awful physical feelings which come with it. These feelings can make us even more anxious, but our logical thinking brain has been cut out of the loop, so cannot help us evaluate the danger in a logical way. This little toddler is trying to protect you, but if you don't really need protecting, you need to help it to reset.

> *When we are calm, the amygdala is calm and information flows to the prefrontal cortex, so we can make better decisions.*

The Smoke Alarm

This brings us to another important aspect to understand about the amygdala. It can't tell the difference between real danger and perceived danger. In her wonderful book for young children *Hey Warrior,* Clinical Psychologist Karen Young compares this to a smoke alarm which responds the same way to a fire as to smoke from burnt toast. It can be helpful to remind our children of this fact.

👍 **Give it a Try!**

After a period of anxiety when things have resolved (never during!) it can also be useful for our children to use this distinction to consider how anxious they have been about a perceived threat. For example, say your child has been worried all week about going to a birthday party on Saturday. Maybe the birthday boy is not in his close friendship group, and his best friend isn't invited. All week he worries about whether he should go. Will he know anyone there? Will he be OK mixing with this unknown group of children? You persuade him to be brave, to give it a try, and he ends up enjoying himself. The following day you might ask him this question about his previous anxiety, "Was the house burning down, or was it just burnt toast?" It can help children see that the events they were so worried about were not so important in the bigger scheme of things.

The smoke alarm analogy in another context can be useful to describe how children respond to anxiety.

🐴 From the Horse's Mouth

Imagine your smoke alarm goes off in your kitchen. Your child (who doesn't struggle with anxiety) hears the alarm from the other room. She may well wait to see if the alarm continues for a little while before responding. If it does, she will come running into the kitchen, to see what's happening. She will assess the situation, and perhaps realise you have just burned some toast. She is reassured there is no real risk of fire and grabs a tea towel, flapping it in the air to re-set the alarm. This is similar to how we respond to anxiety. We respond to our internal alarm, we evaluate the situation, assess the level of risk, and once we recognise that the perceived danger is manageable, we reset our alarm.

However, for some children, it is as if their alarm is set a little too sensitively. Now, imagine your child who struggles with anxiety hears your smoke alarm. This time, she won't delay, she will respond on alert at the very first sound. She will run into the kitchen and see the toast smouldering in the toaster. She might start to feel some reassurance, but then it is as if she has difficulty evaluating the level of risk. She thinks to herself, "Hold on, that toast is still smouldering. It could go on fire at any moment. I'm not really sure we are safe." This time, the child's assessment of the problem is not quite as accurate as the previous example. She might get a tea towel and flap it in the air to re-set the alarm, but she is only flapping half-heartedly as she is still convinced there could be danger. It is as if her whole system is a little off kilter. Her initial response to the alarm, her evaluation of the situation, and her final reaction, are all heightened. This is what it is like for our children who struggle with anxiety.

The Hippocampus aka The Helpful Hippo

If you are explaining this system to children, they will often ask, why me? Why, when my brother is so laid back he is almost hor-izontal, and my sister never seems to worry about much, do I feel so anxious? If we all have the same system in our brains, why am I struggling in this way? This brings us to another important part of this system - the *Hippocampus*. The role of the hippocampus is to process information, organise and retrieve memories.

💡 Top Tip!

I suggest young children imagine her to be a little helpful hippopotamus. Imagine her sitting beside the little amygdala with a note pad in front of her. When the little toddler responds to danger and starts to panic, it is as if she makes a note of that situation, "Oh, that looks dangerous, we must remember that," or "I didn't like the look of that situation. Make a note to be more careful next time." She is storing away our memories and making sure we can retrieve useful information later.

But this is in fact making us more fearful. The children whose amygdala seems a little more sensitive, have these messages reinforced by the hippocampus.

 From The Horse's Mouth

Think about the experience of going on a rollercoaster. Say a child loves the experience. They scream with excitement on the ride, wave their hands in the air, and love the adrenalin. They come off the ride to their dad waiting for them. They might run right past him, shouting that they are going to queue up again for another ride. Their experience and memories of the ride are fantastic.

Now, let's take another child who is terrified by the experience. He comes off the ride, and meets his dad waiting for him. He tells him it was the most terrifying experience he has ever had. His belt was loose, it could have come off at any time, and he could have been flung from the ride. The car nearly shot off the ride as it reached the top of the hill and he was sure the noise he heard was the sound of the bolts loosening. He insists he is never going on the rollercoaster again.

Imagine his dad persuades him to try the bumper cars. The child might consider giving it a try but could transfer his bad experience to the less scary ride. He may see similarities between the two rides, and he may struggle with the idea of feeling safe on either of them. It is as if a negative loop occurs as the hippocampus stores negative memories of being anxious, and then the amygdala becomes more anxious about this and similar experiences.

These two children have gone through the same ride but have experienced it very differently.

The Neural Pathways aka The River

Functional changes in our brains occur when we learn new things and take in new information. These changes are what we call *Neuroplasticity*. This means that the connections in our brains which are used more often become more embedded.

 The Science Bit!

The human brain is made up of an estimated 100 billion neurons making a total of 100 trillion neural connections. When our brain cells communicate frequently, the connections between them strengthen. The pathways in the brain that are used again and again begin to transmit faster and faster, and stronger neural pathways are formed.

If we imagine these pathways working in a similar way to a river developing, it starts with little tributaries high in the mountains. As they grow, they join together and become a trickling stream. These small streams meet and grow larger until they become a strong river. This is similar to how the pathways in the brain become more embedded. Our children's brains are very flexible which means they can be changed. The concept of use it or lose it applies to the neural pathways which are not used. They are eventually reduced. If we think of the river, and we prune back these little tributaries by blocking them with dams, they start to run dry. As we dry up the water course, the riverbed will become smaller and the edges will eventually become overgrown with plants again. If we support our children to cope with danger, to face their fears, and ride the wave of their anxiety, we are helping the neural pathways in their brains to adapt and change.

Some Things That Don't Help

Living in this state of fight or flight is exhausting. Our children are living in a highly stressed state and this makes it harder for them to function in their daily lives. They struggle with decision making, communicating and expressing themselves, and responding in a calm way. These children need our love and support to help them find strategies to cope with their anxiety.

In our attempt to support them, there are some common traps we fall into.

 From the Horse's Mouth

Notice I am using the word *we* here because we all do it. If my husband was writing this book, he would call this section *Everything Mary has tried and learned didn't work,* so please if you can relate to these things don't feel you are alone. These are our natural responses to our children's anxiety.

Don't Worry Be Happy

The first mistake we often make is to reassure the child that there is no need to be anxious. Have you ever heard yourself saying, "Don't be silly. It'll be grand," or "There is absolutely nothing to worry about." This doesn't work.

We know there is nothing to worry about, so we assure them that there is nothing to worry about. Your anxious child would love to believe you, but their brain is in overdrive. You are appealing to that higher-level thinking area of the brain but remember that little warrior is in control.

> *We have all heard the saying, no-one has ever calmed down by being told to calm down. Well it's true!*

Avoid Reinforcing Fears

We also sometimes unintentionally reinforce our children's fears. Although we don't want to belittle a child's anxiety, we don't want to amplify it. For example, your child is frightened of dogs, and you show anxiety yourself if you see a dog approaching and rush your child in the opposite direction. In this way, we are giving our child more reason to believe there is something to be anxious about.

Linked to this is trying to over-prepare our children. Sometimes we talk about what's ahead far too early. Try instead to keep anticipatory periods short. For instance, thinking about going to the dentist is often worse than the experience! It is not that we don't want to acknowledge their fears, but the message we want to give is one of support.

Instead of amplifying their anxiety, we want to acknowledge it, and let them know we will help them get through this.

Avoid Promises You Can't Keep

In the same manner, we sometimes attempt to reassure our children by guaranteeing them that something will never happen. Unless you are 120% sure something will not happen, don't make a promise you can't keep. For example, a parent told me about her son's first flight on holidays when they experienced severe turbulence. About a week into their holiday her son kept asking when they were due to fly home. He was very anxious that there might be turbulence on the return plane journey, so she guaranteed him that their outgoing flight was a once off and assured him this wouldn't happen on the way home. You can imagine what happened. If you cannot guarantee something won't happen, don't promise it. Your child who is struggling with anxiety needs you as their safe space. They need to know they can trust and believe you.

Avoid Avoidance

Finally, the most important thing to avoid is avoidance itself. Your child will usually want to avoid the situation which causes anxiety. The flight part of the fight or flight response urges you to escape the threatening situation. This is a dangerous approach because it seems to work. Helping children avoid the things they are afraid of will make them feel better in the short term, but it reinforces the anxiety over the long run. The child will never learn that he can cope with this anxiety. As parents we instinctually protect our children from anxiety, so we often allow them to avoid the situations which make them anxious. But by doing this we are inadvertently telling the child that this situation is one they should be fearful of.

 Top Tip!

The best way to help children overcome anxiety isn't to remove all the stressors that trigger it. Instead, it is to support them to face the situations that make them afraid. This will help them to function as well as they can, even when they're anxious, and will result in a long-term decrease in anxiety.

Pushing Beyond the Comfort Zone

I was once told that the comfort zone is a beautiful place, but nothing ever grows there. It rang very true for me, particularly when considering our children who struggle with anxiety. Sitting in our comfort zone is a very anxiety neutral position. We feel calm and safe. Although routine and stability are important for our children, some of them need encouragement to come out of their comfort zone, particularly those who struggle with anxiety. When their decisions are based on fear, they are missing out on many life experiences. They need to find the balance between comfort and risk, and by encouraging them to step out into the world, we help them to persevere with life's challenges. Helping them to take small steps and giving them the support which they need to try new things can help them to build confidence and resilience.

 What Does the Research Say?

A growing body of research has begun to examine the area of 'challenging parenting behaviour' and whether it is a buffer against anxiety in children. Challenging parenting behaviour includes behaviour such as encouraging children to take risks; encouraging them to explore unfamiliar situations with confidence; encouraging children to be assertive; and to engage in rough and tumble play. One international research study from Macquarie University[28] found that children of parents who helped them push boundaries were less likely to struggle with anxiety disorders. The researchers concluded by recommending that parents should encourage their children to push their limits.

This is something I know that I, and many other parents, battle with. Often the first thing our children will ask us to do is to help them to overcome anxiety by removing stressors. Instead we need to support our children to function as well as they can, even when they are anxious. We can challenge ourselves to display confidence in our children, particularly when we or they are feeling anxious about a situation. By encouraging them to take reasonable risks and gently pushing their limits we are helping them to find the courage to face their anxieties. Every time they are brave and push through their anxiety, they are building confidence in the world and strengthening the connections in the brain that support this brave behaviour.

If we do not gently push our children out of their comfort zones, avoidance becomes their go to response to anxiety. There is a very real danger that the child will shrink away from the world, and retreat into the safety of their home, or the safety of their room. Clearly that is not what we want for our children.

We cannot tell them that life is always safe, but we can tell them that when they are trying to find their inner brave we will be there with them, supporting them. Anxiety and bravery are inextricably linked, but often the anxious child forgets that. Our children who struggle with anxiety are brave every single day of the week.

Sometimes just getting out of bed in the morning to face the world takes bravery. Reminding them of the strength they have internally, will encourage them to see it too while also equipping them with tools to help them to be brave when they don't feel it. Remember, it is we who are the most important tool they have to help them cope with the anxiety they are feeling. It is their connection with us that helps to give them the strength they need to face their fears.

It Takes a Village

I have three kids, 10, 5 and 2 years old, and every day of these 10 years I have wondered am I doing it right? Tonight I got my answer. My 10-year-old son loves me to lie beside him at night and talk about his day, and sometimes I lie there while he goes to sleep. He was holding my hand while dozing off and said, "Mummy, I love when you lie with me because I feel like all my worries disappear and I feel so safe." That was the moment I knew I was doing something right. It's definitely moments like that that bring me back to the reality of what it's all about.

[Credit: Sinead Connolly, via Facebook]

In addition to our support, providing the tools that will help them to breathe through those anxious moments until they understand how brave they are, will encourage them to see the benefits of moving beyond that comfort zone.

90 Second Rule and Controlled Breathing

The *90 Second Rule* is a term coined by Dr Jill Bolte Taylor in her book *My Stroke of Insight*[29] to explain the lifespan of negative emotions. She advises that when we react to something in our environment, this sets off a 90 second chemical process within our body during which we cannot control these reactions. Following this 90 second period, these chemicals are flushed out of our bodies. She argues that after that time, the remaining emotional and ongoing physiological response is down to our own reactions to the situation.

If we can watch this process, feel it happening, but respond in a calming way, this will result in those responses leaving our bodies. Easier said than done you might say!

By pausing in that moment and using our breathing to send calming messages back to our brains, we are stopping our thoughts from re-stimulating the fight or flight response in our brains. This is important when we consider our children's anxiety, as after that 90 second delay, we are in a position to influence how we respond to the fight or flight instinct.

 What Does the Research Say?

Controlled breathing is scientifically proven to counter the stress response and is one of the most important tools we can teach our children to use in order to breathe through anxious moments. If our children practice controlled breathing, these deep, controlled breaths can slow the heart rate, lower blood pressure, and calm the fight or flight response set off by the amygdala.

Controlled breathing is just breathing, right? Well not exactly. Most of us don't really think about how we are breathing. We just breathe. But if you stop for a moment and watch yourself breathing in a mirror, many of us, particularly those who are anxious, will find that we are breathing into our upper lungs. You will probably see your upper chest expand and your shoulders move. This type of breathing is our go-to response when we are anxious. But what we should be aiming for is breathing down into our diaphragm, taking even, deep breaths, resulting in the air moving to our lower lungs. We usually call this *belly breathing* when speaking to children. This is the most efficient way to breathe. It starts in the nose and moves down into the stomach as the diaphragm contracts, and your lungs fill with air. Humans are naturally belly breathers. If you watch a young baby breathing, you will see them breathe down into their belly. By deliberately shifting our breathing in this way we can stimulate the body's relaxation response, which is a calming influence.

👍 Give it a Try!

How do we breathe in this way?

- First, get comfortable. You can either stand or lie down.
- Place one hand on your chest and the other on your stomach.
- Start by taking a normal breath, and exhale.
- Then inhale slowly through your nose, taking the breath down into your stomach, allowing your chest and stomach rise as you fill your lungs. You should feel the hand on your stomach rise.
- Pause for a moment, then breathe out slowly through your mouth, and repeat. These breaths should be slower and deeper than you usually take.
- Continue this breathing pattern for about three to five minutes, breathing gently into the lower lungs and expanding your abdomen. Let your breath flow as deep as is comfortable without forcing it.

  You need to practice this calming breath on a regular basis. If you started practicing when lying down, move on to practicing it at other times during your day. This controlled breathing encourages full oxygen exchange, slows the heartbeat, and can help stabilise blood pressure.

Breathing Buddies

Breathing Buddies - a little stuffed cuddly toy or bean filled toy - are a great way for children to practice controlled breathing.

Children lie comfortably and place their breathing buddy on their stomach. They then focus on the breathing buddy moving up and down as they slowly inhale and exhale. Doing this helps them to breathe down into their diaphragm. Get them to inhale through their nose for a count of three, down into their tummy until they see the breathing buddy move. Pause for a moment, then exhale for a count of three, pause for a moment, then repeat the process. If your child struggles to focus, you can get him to silently say *in* to himself as he breathes in, and *out* to himself as he breathes out. This can help younger children maintain a focus on the exercise.

Explain to your child how this way of breathing sends the message back to their amygdala that all is well. It is also a way of showing your child that their breathing is within their own control. Doing this exercise helps children calm down, focus, and helps them understand that paying attention to their breathing can help them relax when they are feeling anxious.

💡 Top Tip!

With older children you might want to use a flat stone instead of a cuddly toy on their stomach. As with the breathing buddy, you ask them to focus on the stone moving up and down as they breathe. Teenagers can try the exercise standing up, with one hand placed on their chest, the other on their abdomen.

Whatever their age, if you get your children to practice this on a regular basis, every night before bed, and again as part of their regular daily routine, it becomes a learned behaviour. The more regularly your child practices this breathing, the more able they will become at putting it into practice when they need it.

Although there is no magic wand to wave away our children's anxiety, awareness of the 90 Second Rule and controlled breathing is important in terms of our ability to respond to stress.

The provision of simple interventions such as controlled breathing exercises have the capacity to shape the emotional wellbeing of our children, helping them deal with their anxiety. Once they know this technique, and have practiced it, then we can help support them in moving out of their comfort zones.

Other Practical Relaxation Tools

There are various techniques you can use when encouraging relaxation in children who are struggling with anxiety or emotional regulation. A parent once told me she was constantly telling her young son to calm down before she realised he had no idea how to even begin to do this! If we want our children to calm or to use a tool to cope when they are feeling stressed or anxious, we need to spend the time in giving them some age appropriate tools to use.

Glitter Jars

Glitter jars were developed initially for children who struggle with self-regulation but can be equally useful for children dealing with anxiety, or any stressful situation. A glitter jar is a glass jar filled with water, clear glue, and glitter. If angry or upset the child shakes the jar and the glitter swirls, representing their feelings. Children can sit and relax while doing their belly breathing and watch the glitter as it swirls until it settles on the bottom of the jar. The glitter represents everything going on inside their heads, inside their hearts, and inside their bodies. As they breathe slowly, the glitter settles just like their feelings.

👍 **Give it a Try!**

To make a glitter jar at home, clean off the outside of the jar and ask the child to choose coloured glitter to place in the jar. They can choose colours to represent their emotions – red for anger, green for jealousy, purple for anxiety and so on. They can also add in larger sequins to represent the things they have in life to ground them, for example a sequin could represent a parent, a grandparent, or even a pet. These larger sequins will settle to the bottom more quickly than the smaller glitter pieces and remind the child of the good things they have in their life, as they are breathing. When making the jar, remember to add the clear glue, as it helps with the swirling motion. Also use hot water when making the jar initially. It is a good idea to glue the lid back onto the jar to avoid leaks.

I cannot stress enough the benefits of these jars. The glitter is such a concrete representation of what the child is feeling, and watching the glitter settle as they breathe deeply, is such a positive strategy for the child to use when they want to address their anxiety, or indeed any strong emotion.

🐴 **From the Horse's Mouth**

A student of mine told me about a particular boy in her preschool class who she felt would really benefit from a glitter jar. She made the jars in class and demonstrated how to use them to the children. As expected, this boy was using his jar quite often. She would see him glaring at his friend if they had an argument, and then march over to his glitter jar, glaring back at his friend the whole way.

Then sometimes she would see his friend glare back, then march over to his glitter jar. She said it was like something from a cowboy film in the beginning with these two four-year-olds having a stand-off, both furiously shaking their glitter jars at each other! But soon they learned the benefit of breathing out their anger and frustration, and the glitter jars did their work.

Body Scan

Another tool is a squeeze and release *Body Scan* which involves practicing tensing and relaxing different muscles in the body to induce calm. It also helps children to recognise the difference between feeling tense and being relaxed.

👍 Give it a Try!

To learn this technique, ask your child to lie down with their arms by their sides. Encourage them to allow their body to relax and close their eyes. Take three deep breaths. Then as they breathe in, concentrating on their toes only, ask them to squeeze them as tight as they can. Then as they exhale, release and relax their toes. Move to their feet. Squeeze them as they inhale, then release as they exhale. They continue to move up through their body, bit by bit, tensing and releasing each part as they slowly breathe in and out. With each body part, get them to focus on the tension as they squeeze and release. When they have scanned their whole body, ask them to take three deep breaths and slowly open their eyes.

With practice this method helps the child to have an awareness of their body, and the tension contained within it. Don't be surprised if they fall asleep the first time they try it! After the scan you can talk to them about how it felt to tense up, and how it felt to release. Finally ask them, now that they have gone through the exercise, does their body feel more tense or more relaxed. The idea is that they start to recognise the sensations within their body, and how strong emotions can impact on them in physical ways. If you are doing this at bedtime, do it before your controlled breathing. I always suggest the controlled breathing should be the last exercise before bedtime.

The Worry Box

Another useful tool is to create a worry box for children to put their worries in or to create a daily ritual of *worry time* with your child, when they talk about their worries. This can be something you do every day, maybe more than once a day at the beginning, but over time, you may well not need to do it as often.

I usually recommend that worry time can take place when the child comes in from school (after they have been fed and watered!) and again in the evening. Try not to do it last thing at night. If you want to do it as part of the bedtime routine, do it before bath and story time. Then after those times, leave your body scan or controlled breathing exercises till last thing at night.

👍 Give it a Try!

During worry time encourage your children to release all their worries. You can write them down or your child can draw them and put them into a worry box, or you can just talk about them, depending on the age and preference of the child. Young children often like to make a worry box which they can decorate themselves. Older children might prefer to write worries on post-it notes and put them in a worry jar or write them in a journal. During worry time anything, no matter how small it seems, constitutes a valid worry.

However, worry time is limited! The idea is to stop the child from spending the whole day ruminating over their worries, but to get them used to the idea of focusing on them for a short while instead. It may be a 10, 15 or 20-minute period of time, but when the time is up, close the box and say good-bye to the worries for the day.

Say you have worry time with your child after they have come in from school. You talk through their worries, and maybe you write them down and put them in their worry box. Then later you are making dinner, and your child comes running up with some worries they had forgotten to tell you about earlier in the day. You want to try to stop the whole evening becoming worry time, but you also don't want to dismiss the child's worries. So, you can say something like, "Oh it sounds as if that was hard for you. I really want to hear all about that. Will you make sure you save that one and tell me all about it at worry time? But could you help me now with peeling those carrots, and I will remember to ask you all about that worry later." The child knows you are acknowledging the worry, but you want to focus on something else now. It sounds a little bit harsh to start with, but if you have a child who tends to dwell on their worries all day long, it is so much better for them to slowly get used to limiting the time they spend in this way. The aim is to reduce the time spent on worry time, and perhaps move it to once a day. You are not dismissing their worries but empowering the child by teaching them that they can postpone some of their worries till later.

Top Tip!

If the child finds they are dwelling on their worries all day in school, you can ask them to imagine they are putting the worry into a worry box in their mind. This allows them to save it for worry time at home while they are freed up to do something else in school. It can be hard to wait for worry time, but after a while, they will find they can't remember all the little worries of the day.

At the end of worry time, when your worries have been talked about, maybe written down, and placed in your worry box or jar, it can be good to shift the focus. To do this, at the end of worry time I recommend briefly making a note or thinking about three things your child was grateful for that day. It might be their teacher, it might be chatting with grandad, or it might be spending time playing with their dog. It helps to round off worry time by acknowledging some of the good things in their life.

Build a Fear Ladder

We know from the above that avoidance is the go-to response for many children to their anxiety, and one of our goals as parents should be to help them avoid avoidance. Two techniques which are particularly useful in supporting our children to slowly move out of their comfort zones are the *Step Ladder Approach* and the *Imagined Edge*. Both of these approaches stem from the idea of gradual exposure, which means facing your fears in a step by step way. Rather than avoiding situations which make your child anxious or advising them to jump in the deep end and risk the child becoming completely overwhelmed, this involves starting with a situation which provokes the least amount of anxiety and slowly moving towards more challenging situations. It is basically a step by step approach to climbing the ladder of anxiety, breaking the task into manageable pieces, and using gradual exposure to reach a goal.

The Step Ladder

Before you start, you need to talk to the child about the process and how it works. Along with your child you picture a simple step ladder with several rungs. With younger children they can draw a step ladder, so they have a concrete image to work with. Together you decide on the final goal, and this task becomes the top of the ladder. The first step becomes the starting point - ideally a situation which causes your child the least anxiety. Together you agree on the individual small steps to take to reach the goal, with each one a little more challenging than the previous step. It is important that the tasks on each step of the ladder are not too daunting. The idea is that although the child is facing a greater challenge with each step, these are manageable and will result in them developing more confidence as they slowly proceed through each step. Anxiety will drop over time as you go through the laddering process. It might not drop to zero. It will take time, but the process can really help a child to manage their anxiety and get over their fears.

Before the child takes the first step, it is important to teach them strategies for managing anxiety, such as controlled breathing mentioned above. Practise this with your child before starting so he knows what to do as soon as he starts to feel anxious. Encourage your child to stay in the situation until his anxiety has passed. The child will feel uncomfortable, but by staying in the situation they are confirming they are brave enough to handle it.

👍 Give it a Try!

Here is an example of the Step Ladder for a little girl who has separation anxiety and does not want her mother to be out of her sight.

Step 1: She plays in her room while mum sits reading in the corner.

Step 2: She plays in her room while mum is in the adjoining room.

Step 3: She plays in her room while mum is cleaning the bathroom.

Step 4: She plays in her room while mum is downstairs.

Step 5: She plays in the house while mum puts the washing on the line.

Step 6: She stays home with dad while mum nips to the shop.

Step 7: She stays home with dad while mum goes out for lunch.

Step 8: She says home with granny while mum and dad go to lunch.

Step 9: Granny babysits while mum and dad go out for the evening.

Step 10: Granny babysits for the day while mum and dad go out.

Step 11: She goes to a friend's house to play for an hour.

Step 12: She goes to a friend's house to play for the afternoon.

The idea is that each step presents a challenge for the child which may cause some anxiety but is manageable. Some steps might prove more challenging than others and might need a longer timespan to achieve. Most steps will need to be practiced for some time before they become manageable. But the parent would recognise that each step, no matter how small, represents an achievement.

Anxious feelings don't last forever, our bodies will only maintain high levels of anxiety for a short time. It may well take some time for the child to feel ready to progress through each step - when it no longer results in anxiety. Don't force the pace, instead encourage them. You want them to feel a sense of mastery as they accomplish a step.

Move at the speed of trust. Remember to offer lots of praise each time your child achieves a step on the ladder. Remind them they are showing real bravery each time they overcome another step in the process.

Facing these fears show the child they can cope with more than they previously believed possible. They also come to understand that the breathing techniques they have learned really can help them to cope in stressful situations. Finally, they gain a real sense of achievement as they progress up the ladder and face their fears.

The Imagined Edge

Similar to the *Step Ladder* approach, is an even more gentle approach called *Think It, Feel It, Do It* involving the *Imagined Edge*. This is a technique outlined by Lawrence Cohen in his wonderful book, *The Opposite of Worry*[30]. Cohen starts by outlining his version of the *Subjective Units of Distress Scale* - a scale from 0-100 used in psychology to rank intensity levels of distress. He presents a smaller scale of 0-10 for children which he calls a *Fear-O-Meter*. The scale should be individual to the child and represent how low or high their anxiety levels feel. Parents should agree the wording of this scale with their child. For example, 0 might represent a piece of cake; 5 might represent getting tough; and 10 might represent about to explode with anxiety. Once the scale is agreed (and for younger children, drawing a picture of the scale can be a good idea) you ask the child, "What is your number right now?" The child identifies where they are on the scale at that point in time. This scale is also a useful way to measure the effectiveness of any anti-anxiety technique, by asking the child what their number is before and after using their controlled breathing for example.

The idea is that the child vividly imagines the step which causes them anxiety (Think It). This pushes them to experience the same anxiety as if they were facing it in real life (Feel It). After repeatedly doing this they are ready to face the task in real life (Do It).

As with the Step Ladder approach, parent and child agree a hierarchy of situations which cause anxiety. The child starts to vividly imagine the lowest level situation, and the parent asks, "What is your number right now?" At that point the child might be at a seven. They then do their controlled breathing (or another anxiety lowering technique if preferred). After a while the parent asks for their number, which would be expected to be lower down the scale. The process is repeated over and over, with the child moving up and down the scale, but with each repetition, their anxiety about that specific thought is lowered. To use an example of a child who cannot bring themselves to go to school, the first step might be to imagine getting up in the morning and putting on their school uniform. The next step might be to imagine packing their schoolbag, lunch etc, and leaving the house for school. The next step might be driving to school and standing in the yard, and so on. When each level stops raising the number on the Fear-O-Meter, your child is ready to try imagining the next step on the hierarchy. Over time this process will support the child in facing their anxiety and seeing they have tools to enable them to cope in stressful situations.

The Science Bit!

If you remember the neural connections I mentioned earlier, this process can have an impact on them. We know the amygdala cannot tell the difference between real danger and perceived danger. It responds the same way to these imagined situations as it would to the real-life experience. By doing these exercises we are setting up the neural pathways to adapt to these anxiety provoking situations. It is important to tell the child that every time they think these brave thoughts, and face their fears, they are strengthening the areas of the brain that will help them to ride the wave of their anxiety.

The Second Chicken

One of our goals as parents is to support our children to become autonomous adults. Our children live in very demanding times, but have we as parents prepared them for those demands? We have already discussed the locus of control, which refers to our beliefs about the level of control we have over life events. Having an externalised locus of control results in our children feeling they have limited power over their lives. We need to consider our role as parents in promoting a strong sense of control in our children in terms of supporting them to cope with anxiety.

What Does the Research Say?

A book published in 2018, *The Coddling of the American Mind*[31], investigates why rates of mental illness in American college students are steadily rising. It states, more than 50% of college students said they felt overwhelming anxiety in the previous twelve months. Although they cannot prove causation, the authors link this to the rise of fearful parenting. They argue that teenagers today are treated like candles, which can be extinguished by a puff of wind, and sheltered from anything that could cause offence.

I was first introduced to the idea of the second chicken by Clinical Psychologist David Coleman who references the story to Lawrence Cohen in the book I mentioned earlier, *The Opposite of Worry*. Cohen tells the story of how chickens use tonic immobilisation, basically freezing and playing dead, when under threat by predators. If a chicken fears threat it will play dead for about a minute. However, Cohen found that if that chicken sees a second chicken who also fears threat, the two chickens will play dead for up to five minutes. It is as if the first chicken thinks to himself, "Well if that chicken thinks something is wrong, I must be missing something, so I better play dead for longer." However, if the second chicken is walking around happily, the first chicken pops back up very quickly. This time it seems to think, "Well, if that guy thinks everything is OK, it must be OK." A scared chicken looks to the second chicken to see if the world is safe. Cohen found that chickens stayed immobilised for longest when they looked in a mirror and thought that their own frozen reflection was another scared chicken!

He relates this to children who struggle with anxiety and the responses of their parents. I suppose the question to ask ourselves as parents is, "How can we make sure we are not that scared second chicken?"

👍 Give it a Try!

Even if we reassure our child that nothing is wrong, as we noted earlier, logic will not work when a child is in a state of heightened anxiety. Instead Cohen suggests we use the *Second Chicken Question.*

- *"Would you look in my eyes and see whether or not I'm scared?"*

He suggests this works much better than simple reassurance that everything is fine, as it brings them into the present, and helps them feel your projection of calm confidence.

When our children are anxious, they will look to us for reassurance. If they see us looking anxious it seems to confirm to them that the world is indeed not a safe place, they are right to be scared.

When the world seems a scary place, the most important thing our children need from us is calm. We may not be able to control the world, but we can control our responses. That is where our power lies. Their biggest influence is their connection to us. We can let them know that we are their port in the storm. We cannot promise they will never face challenging situations, but we can let them see our faith in their ability to cope.

Anxiety is felt on a spectrum, although it is natural to feel some anxiety, for some children it becomes something they really struggle with. It is normal for children to have some fears and worries, however some anxious children may need greater support. **Please always see your GP if you feel your child's anxiety is a problem which is significantly affecting their daily life.**

CHAPTER 7

THE ONLINE CHILD - WELLBEING
AND DIGITAL PARENTING

---

*It's time to move beyond the conversation about 'screen time' and
talk instead about the interplay between technology and wellbeing.
Speaking about screen time is like speaking about 'food time' or
'book time.' No one ever says, "How much food time have you
had?" A more productive conversation is to talk about what kids
are doing on their screens rather than how long they're
staring at pixels.*

Dr Justin Coulson

Parenting in the Digital Age

Teenagers today are the first generation to grow up with a mobile
device in their hands, and as parents, we face the challenge
of managing their use of digital media. We sometimes call these
children *Digital Natives* as they are native speakers of the language
of technology[32]. As for the rest of us, the oldies who were introduced
to the digital world later in our lives, we are *Digital Immigrants*.
We speak a different language to the younger population, and this
can cause us to make assumptions about how our children use

technology. We forget sometimes as parents, that this is an area in which they can teach us a thing or two!

In 2019, CyberSafe Ireland conducted a survey of almost 4,000 Irish children, between age eight and thirteen years, about their online activity[33]. *92% owned their own smart device and were active online.*

Technology is an integral part of the way our children live. There are real benefits for them from certain types of online activity. Firstly, it exposes them to a wealth of information which can build their knowledge and experience. There is a vast array of educational activities available online. Our children can learn almost anything using technology, from cookery to guitar lessons to learning a new language, and many of these are free to use.

For young children there is support for developing literacy and numeracy skills through a huge array of educational games and apps. Some of these also teach our children about teamwork and social skills such as empathy and co-operation. Some practise turn-taking and cooperation, while there are many creative benefits via apps which involve imagination or art.

Research has shown students who conduct research online re-tain what they have researched for much longer than the knowledge gained through traditional learning. I cannot imagine the number of times my children have asked me about something from their homework and I have told them to Google it! Being online can help children become more creative, develop academically and can ex-pand their world view.

For tweens and teens, they can develop their writing and critical thinking skills by writing blogs or develop their political and social awareness watching current affairs and documentaries on YouTube.

Computer games can also help them develop problem-solving and critical thinking skills. Technology can also make children feel less isolated as it takes away physical barriers to connecting with friends and family who may live a distance away.

Rather than dismiss technology, we should appreciate the benefits. Having said all that, most parents would agree that different aspects of technology are more suitable for different age groups, and we need to consider the benefits of what they are doing.

How Old to Start?

Most of the research would recommend we aim for no screen time for children under two years old, with some studies finding a relationship between handheld device use and language delays in young children.

 It takes a Village

I have to admit that it is the saddest sight for me, when I see a toddler trying to swipe the pages of a book, or the television, or worse still, expertly using a phone or tablet. Yes, technology is a wonderful thing when used responsibly, but leave the little ones to learn like they should, without screens...let them be little.

[Credit: Alex Koster, via Facebook]

For children over two, it is recommended parents engage in screen time along with the child, so you are exploring together. Viewing should be limited to age appropriate sites with high quality programming, where parent and child are talking about what they are watching. We are aiming for an interactive process. It is easy for those of us with older children to scream we would never let our children within six feet of a screen if they were still this age. However, if we are realistic, we know sometimes we use technology to keep our children occupied for short periods. If a parent, on occasion, uses their phone to keep a child entertained while they take a few minutes to get something done, it is not going to cause any long-term harm. But the aim is to avoid it as much as is possible.

When our children reach school age, there is a vast range of age appropriate material available to them online. We need to bear in mind that all technology is not created equal. It is important to consider how they engage, and what they are engaging with. It is best to limit their usage to sites you feel are suitable for your individual child. There are plenty of online tools and parental control options to restrict access to their viewing. It is also a good idea to avoid using technology close to bedtime, as research tells us it can interfere with sleep.

In terms of social networking sites, the majority only allow users aged thirteen and over. Most of these were never designed with child users in mind, however, we know children younger than thirteen are signing up to these sites.

 What Does the Research Say?

CyberSafe Ireland report that 92% of eight to thirteen-year-olds are active online. Almost half of these have spoken to people they do not know in real life via social media and gaming platforms, some doing so at least once a week. A high number also report playing over 18s games and being exposed to violent and sexual content online.

These findings suggest many of us need to do a better job of monitoring screen time and making sure it is balanced with other aspects of life.

Time Spent Online

The amount of time young people spend online has doubled in the past decade. In the UK, Ofcom report that tablets are the devices most likely to be used by children from 3-15, with children reporting that they often watch TV and YouTube on these devices.

 What Does the Research Say?

International research published in 2019 by Common Sense Media[34] explored the impact of this time spent on smartphones and other mobile devices, specifically looking at how it has changed families' routines and in-person relationships. Focusing on teens and their families in the UK, the research noted that although there was an optimism about the benefits of mobile technology, both teens and parents felt mobile devices were daily distractions in family life. Many teens reported feeling addicted to their technology and highlighted technology usage as an emerging source of conflict within families. Younger children spent on average five hours a day on screens, while for teens this rose to almost seven and a half hours.

These findings are incredible when you consider most children are at school for seven hours from Monday to Friday. To put some of this into perspective, we are told the average teen consumes more than 10,000 messages a day via social media, phones, and television. Wow!

How do parents feel about the amount of time their children spend online? The Common Sense Media report noted a growing awareness among parents about their children's over-reliance on their phones.

One in five of us argue with our children about device use on a daily basis.

The majority of parents in the study felt monitoring their children's media use is important for their safety, with parents of tweens most likely to check their children's devices. In addition to monitoring, most parents reported having a range of rules around technology in their homes. The most common rule being mobile devices were not allowed during family meals, or bedtime. Parents ranked family conversations highest on a list of activities negatively affected by mobile device use. It was clear from the research that mobile devices were having a major impact on family life.

If we are honest with ourselves most of us have used technology at some point to occupy our children while we get even a small bit of time to do something, or to have a little headspace. It is unrealistic to say we will never allow our children to engage with technology. In fact, this would not be in their best interests considering, as we discussed above, there are many benefits. Technology is very much a part of modern life. However, we need to consider *how* they engage with it.

👍 **Give it a Try!**

Rather than demand your child blindly follows your rules, it can be better to decide on what is most important to you. So, what are your non-negotiables?

- Parents have a right to know passwords?
- Parents have a right to check phones?
- No phones or laptops in bedrooms?
- An agreed time to turn off technology each evening?
- Family computer kept in an open place?
- No phones at the dinner table?
- Technology only to be used for educational purposes?
- A written family code of conduct for technology?

Each family will have different rules regarding technology depending on the ages of their children and their own values.

Once you have decided on the non-negotiables, then you can decide what areas you would consider negotiable. With these in mind, you can sit with your child, talk about the benefits of technology, and your concerns. During this discussion you can agree boundaries together. This should include the length of time the child is allowed online; the time when devices are shut off in the evening; and where the child can and can't use devices. For example, if my primary concern is that computers could make my children more isolated and antisocial, rather than remove the computer I might remove access to the internet alone in their room. Or I might insist the family computer stays in the living room. It is worth starting these discussions as young as possible. As they get older you can relax the rules and agree compromises as you see fit. But continue to have conversations around these areas of concern over time.

Top Tip!

A useful tip for when you want to end a period of screen time, is to make a connection with your child, rather than demand they turn off their device. Sit with them as they use the device, watching along with them. Take a few minutes to start a dialogue about what they are doing on screen and use the conversation to switch their attention. You are entering their world, showing an interest in the activity, then bringing them back to the real world along with you. This is usually a gentler transition than a sudden demand to switch off the device.

Whether your child is constantly checking their social media or watching YouTube videos, taking time to understand their viewing and what it means to them can also help you to stay connected to them. You may find your son, who is constantly watching YouTube videos, is learning to play new guitar tracks by practicing and watching others play. Or your daughter is using social media to stay connected with her friends who she only speaks to in person at the weekend. If you are unsure about a video game they are playing, ask them to teach you how to play it with them. Not only will you have a better understanding of any benefits, but they will have gained from taking on the role of teacher. Having conversations with our children about how they communicate online helps us to take a balanced approach to their viewing.

Common Sense Media also found discrepancies between what we say and what we do. Although parents report they are concerned their children could become addicted to technology, when asked about their own use, on average, including both work and home screen use, their time spent online per day was nine hours! (Although this did include television screens as well as online technology). Despite this, almost 80% of parents questioned said they believed they were good technology role models for their children! It seems we need to learn to practice what we preach.

Three Areas of Concern

Research has identified three primary areas of concern for parents about their child's use of online technology:

- **inappropriate contact**
- **inappropriate content**
- **inappropriate conduct**

Inappropriate contact involves people who children might meet online and includes worries about online predators. Inappropriate content involves unsuitable material children can come across online. Inappropriate conduct involves the conduct of the child themselves, and ensuring they understand they are accountable for what they say and do online.

In terms of inappropriate contact, we all understand the importance of speaking to our children from a young age about the fact that we do not really know who we are dealing with online. It is important we are aware of their privacy settings, and they know to only share information with people they trust.

👍 Give it a Try!

The following checklist should help to identify issues and to open conversations with your child to protect against such contact.

- Never agree to meet anyone you have met online in person.
- Don't give passwords, or personal details to anyone.
- Don't leave accounts public, instead use privacy settings.
- Don't reply to any unwanted or unsolicited messages.
- Don't buy anything without permission, even if it seems to be free.
- Review your list of online friends regularly.
- Use pseudonyms when deciding on usernames.
- Never be afraid to ask for help if you are upset by any online contact.

In terms of inappropriate content, the number one message is that they should come and speak to you if they see or read anything that makes them uncomfortable. For younger children, play alongside them and talk about how to report anyone who says anything mean or nasty. They shouldn't respond to comments or messages that are mean or make them feel uncomfortable. Instead they should tell you, so that you can screenshot messages and block the sender.

As children get older and have more private access to the online world it becomes more likely they could stumble upon inappropriate sites by accident, or via friends. We use age guides for our children's television and cinema viewing, but it is very possible they can come across over-18s content online. Parental control software will help you to filter out violent or sexual content. You can also set search engines to safe mode. Although there are many tools you can use to block access to this material, it is important to speak to your children about the issue. This will lead to better communication and greater honesty long term.

Sometimes a child won't tell a parent about a bad experience they have had online because they fear you might take away their technology. They need to know they can talk about their experiences online with you without the threat of disconnection.

Finally, in terms of inappropriate conduct, they also need to be aware of their personal responsibility. One of the most important rules is, if you wouldn't say it face to face then don't say it online. Would you go up to a stranger in the street and start asking them personal questions? Would you be rude to a stranger in the supermarket if you didn't like what was in their shopping basket? I always tell my children to use the Granny test. If you wouldn't want your Granny to see it, then don't post it online. Teens (and even we as adults) sometimes feel protected by the apparent distance a screen gives you to the real world, but they need to understand that the online world is still the real world. Emphasise the importance of respectful communication online. To avoid offence, we need to be more careful about what we write online than we might be in face-to-face communication.

 What Does the Research Say?

Clinical Psychologist Catherine Steiner-Adair studied how the digital revolution has fundamentally changed our children's lives in her book *The Big Disconnect*[35]. She argues young people's empathy has declined over the past few decades, and this decline is linked to spending too much time online. She believes a lack of social interaction and a move to online interaction by young people has caused their development of empathy and ability to read social cues to be stunted. It seems our children may have to deal with a lot more inappropriate conduct from their peers than we as adults have ever had to deal with from ours.

Having said that, most of us as adults have witnessed, or have been involved in, online discussions which have escalated due to the wording used. Sometimes we use words in jest, or sarcastically, but without face to face contact humour can be lost. Or we can be emotionally impacted by something we read online and respond in haste where our words can be misinterpreted. We should remind our children not to post in anger. Indeed, sometimes it is best not to respond at all. When we are upset or feeling anxious, we can say things we don't really mean. It can help to tell your child about your personal experience of the online world. Share with them any times you have regretted your choice of words in the past, and how you have learned to be cautious. Most of us have learned at some point, and often the hard way, that some conversations are best had offline rather than in a public forum. Also, remind them that content posted online can be easily copied and shared with audiences they can't control. You are allowing people access to information on your thoughts and viewpoints which they can go on to share and can be taken out of context.

As our children become older, they may have greater levels of personal access to technology and the internet. It is normal for them to want some privacy online as they become more independent from us. Remember to keep up the conversations asking about their online experiences. Even with older teens it is worth reminding them every so often about safe internet use. If you have been having these conversations over the years, they should have learned how to exercise their own judgement, and approach technology in a safe and productive way.

iGen: Teenagers and Social Media

We know many of our teens are using social media to extend their social connections. While there are benefits to time spent online connecting with friends, we know there is a relationship between teens who spend more than three hours online and higher levels of depression and anxiety. We cannot prove the direction of this relationship, but it is a question worth discussing. Is technology causing poor mental health or do anxious or depressed teens spend longer trawling through their social media accounts?

What Does the Research Say?

Dr Jean Twenge, Professor of Psychology at San Diego State University, and author of the book iGen², examined surveys of over 11 million teens in America over the past five decades. She found huge differences between iGen (the generation born between 1995 and 2012) and their earlier counterparts.

"The gentle slopes of the line graphs became steep mountains and sheer cliffs," she says. "And many of the distinctive characteristics of the Millennial generation began to disappear. In all my analyses of generational data—some reaching back to the 1930s—I had never seen anything like it." Twenge found that this group view the world differently to earlier generations and spend their teenage years in radically different ways. Why is this the case? 2012 was the year of the most dramatic change, and this was also the year that the proportion of Americans who owned a smartphone surpassed fifty percent. Her belief is that this generation have been radically shaped by their use of smartphones and social media.

In what ways are these teens different to previous generations? From a positive perspective, iGen are physically safer than previous generations. They are less likely to have issues with alcohol and are more likely to be risk adverse. They are less likely to be in a car accident. However, they are less independent than previous generations, taking on adult tasks such as driving or getting a part-time job later in life. They are meeting face to face with their friends less often, instead they are more likely to spend time alone in their bedroom. Twenge argues that iGen teens at 18-years of age act more like 15-year-olds in previous generations.

Worryingly, they are also more psychologically vulnerable than previous generations. They are more likely to say they are lonely and report higher levels of anxiety and depression. Although this generation go out less than their peers, when they do go out, they document every moment of this time online. Unsurprisingly, numbers reporting how they often feel left out has risen rapidly as they watch their friends' world online and at a distance. This is particularly true of girls, with numbers saying they often feel left out almost doubling from 2010 to 2015.

Twenge also identified sleep as an issue. Most of this generation sleep with their phone within reach of their bed. They check social media last thing at night and again if they wake during the night. They use their phone as an alarm clock, meaning it is the first thing they see when they wake. She argues that a lack of sleep is linked to higher levels of anxiety and depression. She also notes levels of teenage suicide in America have dramatically increased since 2011 and describes this generation as being on the brink of the worst mental health crisis in decades.

Twenge has highlighted two factors which may well contribute to these findings. Students in the 1960s mostly felt that personal control was within their grasp, while more recently students predominantly felt life was outside their control. Believing your success in life is within your own control is empowering. If you have a strong sense of control, you have a more internal focus, meaning you feel better prepared to face the world. She also found that this generation are moving from more *intrinsic* goals (such as personal growth, or core values) to *extrinsic* goals (such as public image or financial gain). If my personal satisfaction comes from the views or rewards of others, and I feel I have little control over my own destiny, no wonder my life is more difficult. Twenge argues these two factors correlate significantly with anxiety and depression. She also makes the case that these changes are due to a preoccupation with material gain, and social image. This generation have been repeatedly bombarded with images online which focus on looking good, being popular, and material possessions. From a young age the message has been ingrained in them that success in life depends on popularity, looks, and wealth. They are the generation who value image over substance, and view success as linked to Instagram followers. The image you portray is more important than the person you are.

What can we do to support this generation? Many researchers advocate for limited screen time for our children. Twenge herself suggests under two hours a day as the goal to aim for. Although, she does recognise it is not easy to separate this age group from their phones. There is evidence to suggest that teens who spend more time in non-screen activities are happier. As parents, it is important to encourage activities such as sports and exercise, in-person socialising, and reading print rather than online to promote stronger overall wellbeing.

A Complex Issue

The relationship between technology and children's mental and emotional health may not be as simple as presented above. Much of Twenge's findings have no clear path of causation. In other words, this is her theory, but we have limited proof that smartphone usage causes anxiety or depression. Perhaps iGen are more anxious and depressed and therefore use their phones to a greater extent. Although there has been plenty of research which argues how the widespread use of technology in our children has negative impacts on wellbeing, there is evidence to suggest it is not as simple as this.

 What Does the Research Say?

Research from Oxford University, published in 2019, looks at the social media use of more than 10,000 teens and preteens[36]. The researchers argue that links between social media use and life satisfaction are more nuanced than previous research has suggested. Although digital technology use has a small negative association with adolescent well-being, more so in the case of girls than boys, this study found that other issues also need to be considered. For example, researchers uncovered that the effects of bullying have much larger negative associations with adolescent well-being than technology use. They also found getting enough sleep and regularly eating breakfast have much more positive associations with wellbeing than the impact of technology.

When we examine findings from large-scale studies into social media usage and adolescent mental health, we find that links are small and inconsistent. What we do know is that social media use is more strongly linked to poor mental health if children are losing sleep or being bullied online. In fact, the impact of bullying is about eight times stronger than social media usage. Spending time with friends and getting enough sleep are protective factors for positive mental health in adolescence. We can see that children spending too much time on their phones can miss out on protective face-to-face activities like sport and exercise. However, it is possible that children who are experiencing mental health issues may well have experienced problems even without their phone use.

While it is clear there are claims and counter claims about this issue, there is a general agreement that as screen time goes up, child wellbeing goes down. If psychologists and researchers are still struggling to reach a consensus on the issue, how are we as parents to make our minds up on what the data means? It has been argued we are creating a situation of panic without any real evidence to support it. The jury is still out on this one.

Technology is such an integrated part of our children's worlds. Limiting screen time is fine, but the conversation is much deeper than that. If we want to really inform and educate our children, we need to talk to them about mindful usage and the need for balance in their lives.

Mindful Usage

This leads us to consider if we should switch our focus from monitoring our children's social media to developing a greater understanding of *how* they use their devices. Instead of simply using parental controls, maybe we should look at the emotional effects on our children of engaging online. If, as parents, we consider their usage in terms of their wellbeing, it can help us to support them to have better boundaries around their screen use. This could involve a rule about a balance between on-screen and off-screen time, or maybe a rule about taking one day each week as a screen free day.

 Top Tip!

A useful tip can be to consider what they might add to their day, instead of focusing on what they should cut back on. Instead of saying they can only have so much time after school online, talk to them about other things they might like to do during this time. Maybe time outside with friends, family time, time listening to music, time for exercise, so they are filling their free hours in a more balanced way rather than simply removing their screen time.

If we are considering mentoring our children's use of technology such as social media, we also need to talk to them about some of the potential pitfalls. Firstly, they need to understand the unrealistic representations presented. They are exposed to a constant stream of information implying that happiness depends on the cosmetic. But we can educate them about the pros and cons of social media, and the curated messages they are being exposed to, by encouraging them to approach social media with a critical eye. Talking to them about the people they are following on apps like Instagram and reinforcing the values these people are presenting is a significant discussion needed.

Research shows that the people our teenagers follow on social media makes a real difference. If they follow high-achieving role models it can expand their world view. It helps them understand there is more to life than celebrity culture which they are very much exposed to online. It can be useful to sit with your teen and ask them to show you who they are following online. Rather than insist they un-follow certain celebrities, encourage them to follow some role models with talents and strengths who widen their view. Following positive role models show your teen there are infinite possibilities in life.

There seems to be a growing awareness among older teens, anecdotally more to be seen in girls, about the reality of online activity presenting fake versions of themselves. This is apparent in the number of teenage girls opening a *Finsta* or *Fake Instagram* account, for close friends and family only, where they present a more real version of themselves. These teens show an awareness that there is more to their lives than the 'picture perfect' existence displayed on Instagram and share more realistic versions with those closest to them.

The Science Bit!

Mindful usage of video games is another area worth considering when contemplating teens and tweens. The part of the brain which is responsible for self-regulation is still very much under development in this age group which impacts on their ability to know when to stop playing games online. Combined with this, when our teens are online their brain is releasing dopamine, the pleasure neurotransmitter. This tells our brains that the pleasure we experience is worth seeking out again. This combination means the teenage brain is in pleasure seeking mode, without the benefit of strong self-regulation. We know that technology companies use very persuasive design techniques and reward structures in video games to engage players. As our children's brains are wired to crave instant gratification, unpredictability and a fast pace, this combination can be very addictive. Having said all that, like all other forms of technology, not all gaming is bad, and we need to remember that. Studies have shown that video games can result in the development of other transferrable skills such as enhanced visual perception, strategic thinking, information processing, and multi-tasking.

Once again, not all games are created equal. The effects of different video games have been likened to the effect of eating different foods. The impact of eating a salad is not the same as eating a bar of chocolate!

One of the ways of gaining a better understanding of any game your child is playing, is to play along with them which will help you to assess the benefits or risks.

When I think back to my childhood there were often times of boredom, something our children have so little of. Boredom helps to develop imagination. It helps to cultivate curiosity and increase creativity. We may have complained to our parents we were bored, but in fact these quiet periods gave us time to relax and recharge. Our children have little time to regroup in this way as they are constantly being distracted by their phones and other devices. They need to have time when they unplug from technology every day.

👍 Give it a Try!

In order to develop a more mindful approach to technology, our children also need to know when enough is enough. Time within their day during which they mentally unplug will help them to be emotionally stronger. This time might include:

- a mindfulness activity
- a walk
- playing sports
- gardening
- reading
- listening to music

Whatever works for each individual child. We play an important role in ensuring our children have a balance between online activity and unplugging. Whatever they do while unplugging, the important thing is that the clutter and noise of life is removed for that period.

Having said this, unplugged time is something our children often don't appreciate! They are so connected to their devices that they will usually struggle against this. One of the easiest ways to get around this is to start with some kind of family time when everyone is unplugged. Or have individual unplugged time with each child, but the important thing is that you are giving them your full attention and having quality time with them. This leads us to consider our own relationship with technology.

Looking at Ourselves

Technology enables us to interact in ways we would never have dreamed about in our childhoods. But it can also deprive us of meaningful family connections in our own homes. Steiner-Adair suggests this is the parenting paradox of modern society. Never before has it been easier to connect with others via technology, but we are so distracted by our phones that it can easily impact on our interactions with our children. How often are we so distracted by our phones that our children have to vie for our attention? How often do we stop mid conversation to respond to our phones? How often do we respond to our children's questions without shifting our gaze from our phone screen?

 It Takes a Village

I was in the park last week and watched as a dad pushed his toddler on the swing whilst looking at his phone. I thought then how sad. There was no fun, laughter, joking or messing around.
   [Credit: Judy Evans, via Facebook]

Another international survey of more than 6,000 children about their parent's mobile phone usage found that children were very aware of competing with technology for their parent's attention[37].

More than a third of the children said their parents spent the same or less time with them as they did on their phones. The biggest grievance was parents being distracted by their phones during conversations with their children. I know this really resonated with me as a parent who works from home, and who is reliant on technology to do so.

 From the Horse's Mouth

I use technology every day to enable me to do my job, or various jobs. But does that mean I am exempt to the mammy guilt about using my computer so much? Definitely not!

I remember when I was working on my PhD sitting my children in front of CBeebies while I was trying to finish my thesis. The guilt that I was writing about supporting children's self-esteem, while ignoring my own children, was awful. Many of my students have told me they feel the same guilt as they complete their studies. An awareness of when I am present physically but distracted by technology is something I try to work on. If I am going to be able to help my children put healthy boundaries in place, I know I need to look at my own.

Research on children's language development highlights another issue when considering our interactions with our children. We used to believe that the most important thing in developing children's language skills was the number of words they hear every day. But new research has found that it is *how* parents talk to their children that really counts. Now we talk about what we call *serve and return* conversations. These are an interplay between parent and child and are a simple and powerful way to build a child's brain. Spending one on one time with them while engaging in meaningful conversation really matters. These interactions are like a game of tennis between two participants, where the conversation flows back and forth between the pair. These exchanges provide emotional connections and have also been proven to drive literacy skills regardless of income or education. Making time for these sorts of interactions with our children is all important. This is something we need to ensure we balance with our use of technology. Children learn not only language, but so much more, through these simple yet powerful connections.

 What Does the Research Say?

Recent research by Hunter College New York examined whether the use of mobile phones during interactions with infants would decrease the quality of the exchanges between parent and child, and limit opportunities for in-the-moment interactions, which are so important for child development. The researchers used an adapted version of the *Still Face Paradigm* mimicking typical everyday disruptions to examine the impact of parents distracted by their mobile phones on infant behaviour[38]. They found this unresponsiveness may have negative consequences for children's social and emotional development. They also found that infants of mothers who reported greater levels of mobile phone usage in everyday life showed more negative effects. They argue that parents need to be aware of the impact of being physically present but distracted and unresponsive to their infants.

The message is clear. We need to think about our own use of technology and how it might be impacting on our relationships with our children. When we are with our children, we need to ensure we are more than physically present, but psychologically present too. We are sending out the message that our technology is more important than our relationships; that our phones are what we value most in life. These are very frightening messages for our children. The sad image this research presents is one of parents pulling away from family life, lost in their own screens.

 From the Horse's Mouth

For me, little things like taking time to stop and consider the way I respond to my children when I am working online have helped. Say one of my children comes to ask me a question while I am working at the computer, instead of distractedly answering while facing the computer, which I often used to do, I try to turn away from the screen and face the child when I respond. If I am in the middle of an important document, I may well tell them I need a moment to finish, then I can talk. But when I finish, clicking save on the document, and again turning to face them can help us to connect. If I am looking at my phone and one of them wants to talk, I try to place the phone face down in front of me while I answer, again trying to show them I am giving them my full attention. These are little things, but taking the time to consider how we respond to daily technological distractions in our lives can help us to put in place small but meaningful changes. These can make a real difference in how we connect with our children.

Finally, remember if you are looking at your own social media use, consider the amount of time you are online when in the company of your children, but also *what* you are watching. If we try to become more intentional with our use of technology, we are also sending an important message to our children. If we are mindlessly scrolling through Instagram photos of online influencers, our children are learning from this. However, if we are looking at social media sites with a positive message, and using technology to learn and grow, our children are seeing the positive aspects of online engagement.

👍 Give it a Try!

- Try to keep school mornings technology free. The aim is to focus on our children and connect with them as we all get ready for school.
- Make driving time technology free. Drop off and pick up journeys should be a time to communicate with our children, and to check in on how their day has been.
- Keep mealtimes screen free. These again are opportunities for connection and to bond as a family without the distraction of technology.
- Try to plan some technology free family activities, family board game evenings, family outdoor activities, whatever we feel would suit our own family to strengthen emotional connection.
- Make bedtime rituals a technology free zone. If there is a phone pinging in the background while you are reading a bed-time story, everyone is distracted.

Technology is constantly evolving, as are the risks associated with it. You can reduce these risks by talking to your children about how they communicate online, encouraging them to think critically about the material they access, and to act online in a way they can be proud of. There is a danger that if our children spend too much time in the online world they become over-stimulated, dependent on instant gratification, and overloaded with information. Our children need a balance between what they want and what they need. We can balance this sedentary lifestyle with time for outdoor activity, a good sleep routine, and time for unstructured play opportunities. They need to balance the online world with face to face social interaction with peers.

Limiting screen time is fine, but the conversation needs to be much deeper than that. We need to talk about mindful usage. We also play a role in this as we know to develop emotionally our children need emotionally available parents. We are often digitally distracted ourselves and need to remember to put away our own technology and focus on strengthening our family connection.

CHAPTER 8

CROSSING BOUNDARIES – TEENS AND TWEENS

My teenagers don't always remember that they used to sit in my lap for hours reading books until they fell asleep in my arms, or that I stayed up all night with them when they spiked a fever, or that they used to grab my hand when they were scared. But I hope more than anything when they think about their childhood, they remember the laughter, the joy, and that they were always loved.

Whitney Fleming, Playdates on Fridays

Storm and Stress

Traditionally, adolescence has often been referred to as a time of storm and stress, and a time of turbulence, but is this really the case? Teenagers today are on track to be the most educated generation yet, with many of them staying in education longer than previous generations. They are more connected than any previous generation and have a better understanding of world events. In terms of diversity, they are not as concerned as previous generations about colour, religion, or sexual orientation. For most of their lives there has been a black President in America, and a gay man of Indian descent as Taoiseach in Ireland. They have grown up during a period where women's rights have been at the fore. They have seen 17-year-old Gretta Thunberg campaign for a reduction in carbon emissions, and young activist for female education, Malala Yousafzai, win a Nobel Prize. They have watched as students like Emma Gonzales, Cameron Kasky, and David Hogg, survivors of the Marjory Stoneman Douglas High School shooting, founded the *Never Again* organisation, pushing for stricter gun control laws in the US. They have grown up with issues such as gender, mental health, disability, cultural identity, and equality spoken about around the dinner table. Overall, they have grown up in a society which has seen an extensive change in social thinking and values. The potential within this generation is wonderful!

What Does the Research Say?

Research on social trends[39] has shown this age group are different from previous generations in other ways. They are more likely to mobilise themselves for a variety of causes and believe change should take place via the use of dialogue. They are highly motivated by the search for truth and understand their individual identities. They are more inclusive than previous generations, more aware of social issues, and they highly value the right of self-expression.

We know adolescence is a time of rapid change, during which there are two main aims. The first is to become an independent autonomous adult, and the second is to develop their own identity. How can we best support them to grow into the adults we know they can become, and achieve all they are capable of? Let's start by looking at how their brains are developing.

The Teenage Brain

You may find, as your child goes through their teenage years, it seems as though you are dealing with many familiar issues which you dealt with when they were a toddler. Both developmental stages are times of huge physical, cognitive, emotional, and neurological growth. Just like toddlers, our teens can struggle with impulse control and have a passion for risk-taking.

> *Our toddlers are egocentric, focusing only on their own perspectives and struggling to see situations from another point of view. Again, in the teenage years our children become egocentric. Basically, it is all about me!*

Teenagers often have a heightened belief that everyone is watching them and talking about them, so they are highly self-conscious and attentive to their own appearance and behaviour. They have a need for autonomy and to prove they are independent of us. Just as when they were toddlers, at times they seem immune to our warnings and cautions. It might not feel like it, but this can be a good thing as during both phases they are gaining a sense of identity. From the toddler who is learning they are their own person, to the teen for whom individualisation is part of developing their personal identity.

Sleep is also an issue for both age groups. Our teenagers need long hours of sleep, again linked to this rapid development. But while toddlers may be up at dawn raring to go, your teenager is more likely to go into hibernation late each evening rising at noon.

The Science Bit!

A teenager's biological circadian rhythm is changing. Melatonin, which makes us feel sleepy, is produced in the teenage brain about two hours later than during early childhood. This results in a body clock shift of about two hours, meaning your teen will feel sleepy later than adults, and so often will feel very tired getting up for school in the morning. Although we may think our teen is being lazy lying in bed, they are at the mercy of their hormonal responses!

In the past psychologists believed children's brain development had stabilised before the late teens. We now know that development continues throughout adolescence and on into the 20s. In Western society our children now stay in education for longer, live at home with parents for longer, and are financially supported by parents for longer. All of the above extend the period between puberty and adulthood, and during this time the child changes physiologically, psychologically, and socially. They change from a child into an adult. But these changes may not always run smoothly!

We often say that with teenagers the accelerator is fully working, but the brakes are still in development. Why is that?

The Science Bit!

In terms of brain development, the frontal and pre-frontal lobes are the last part of the brain to develop. This is the area of the brain responsible for executive function. So, abilities such as judgement, insight, empathy, and impulse control are still under development. This growth is slower than the progress of the emotional part of the brain which is well connected at this age and is linked to impulsivity and risk taking. The thinking part of the brain is not yet developed enough to rationalise impulsive behaviour. This is why our teens still struggle with making decisions about risky situations. They are programmed to seek out new experiences, to try new things, and to make lots of mistakes. They are more influenced by peers than parents, but it is less likely that a peer will urge caution, as their brains are changing the same way. So, a peer will more than likely egg a teenager on.

> *The baby and toddler years are physically draining for parents, but the teenage years can be emotionally draining.*

This will ring true for many parents. It can help us to stay sane by keeping in mind that they are not trying to be difficult with all or any of the above, they simply have an awful lot going on developmentally. Let's look at some of the changes they are experiencing and how we can support them through this important time of transition.

Finding Kindred Spirits

Looking at teenage social and emotional development, early attachments with parents and family now shift to a focus on friends and peers who become a particularly important source of information and influence. As teens start to detach from their parents, they also acquire the necessary independence and self-identity to succeed as an autonomous adult. For some children this period of transition can be stressful as it involves increasing levels of responsibility and independence.

 Learning from Psychology

According to psychologist Erik Erikson, the main social task of adolescence is the search for a unique identity[40]. He argues that teens do this by asking the question, "Who am I?" By experimenting with a range of different roles, they should emerge from this stage with a strong sense of self and a feeling of independence and control. If they are not able to engage in personal exploration during this period, he argued, they may remain insecure and confused about themselves and their identity. This reminds us of the importance of gradually allowing our teens more autonomy and control over their lives.

One of the key aspects during this time is to feel a sense of belonging with peers. Some adolescents will go through this period with the support of friends they have known since childhood. But for many this is not the case. Just because they have known a friend since preschool doesn't mean they will be friends forever. During these years our children are still finding out about themselves. Sometimes they find they no longer connect with some of their old friends because they have simply grown apart. During these years they will learn about difference, and the values and principles which develop during this time to make them individuals. These values can mean they grow in different directions, and sometimes if your child and her friend are in a place where they no longer connect, making new friendships can be the right thing to do for both children. Many of our children seek one 'Best Friend Forever' friendship, but during these turbulent years, these are not always easy to find. Our children need to know that friendships can ebb and flow and that there is no perfect friendship. In fact, we might be better to encourage them to have a range of friends from different settings such as school, sports clubs, neighbours and so on. If they are experiencing difficulties with one group, they have others to call on for support.

An issue many of our teens face in today's modern world is feeling excluded as they see photographs of friends online. Before the rise of electronic devices if a child was left out of a group activity, at least they didn't have to witness the event. Today, they can feel excluded as they see their peers together when they haven't been invited along. They live through a blow by blow account of the outing via social media. Sometimes this is orchestrated purposely by the 'so called' friends who have excluded one child from the activity. This can be devastating for a child, and for the parent who is left dealing with the fallout. There is no easy answer to this.

 What Does the Research Say?

Although it could be argued that experiencing exclusion in this way will build resilience, it is hurtful to be excluded and to have it thrown in your face. A recent research project in the US asked teens about how they cope with this type of exclusion and what they would recommend as coping strategies to others[41]. The teens were very familiar with this experience and agreed that it happens all the time. Although they felt everyone has a right to post photos, they admitted it can be very difficult to deal with. The teens were aware that sometimes they wanted to spend time with one group of friends, although some of their other friends would not be included.

In this instance they recommended taking an honest approach, and letting the other friends know they were busy, and by implication out with others, rather than lie about their whereabouts. In fact, the teens were reluctant to admit that posting images was done deliberately to hurt others. We know our teens are very much caught up in their own needs. It is possible that posting is done without any real consideration of the impact on those left out.

Nevertheless, the teens seemed aware of the complexity of their digital lives. Indeed, most had been on both sides of the coin. They had been in a group who had posted photos online without consideration of others but had also been the rejected party who was not included and were aware of the emotional turmoil of being in that situation. They had an overwhelming belief in the rights of their peers to share images but were also clear in their advice to others on how to cope if they were the one being left out.

The overarching message was to make a conscious choice not to ruminate over their exclusion. Instead, they advised the best action was to put in place other soothing practices to make themselves feel better and help them avoid looking at the images online. Most involved spending time with other friends or family instead, and their list of activities which helped included:

Call other friends and invite them over

Spend time with your family

Put away your phone

Watch Netflix

Eat ice cream

Exercise

Making the decision when in this situation to put your phone away, difficult as we all know that is, and instead to proactively reach out to other friends or family, is most definitely a step towards empowerment for these children.

Nonetheless, this is such a difficult issue for parents to deal with, and if issues like this are happening on an ongoing basis, sometimes we may have to challenge them to consider the behaviour of their friends and to question the impact these relationships are having on their lives. They can be kind, but assertive, and sometimes we need to talk to them about what true friendship feels like. They want to be part of the group; they want to be accepted. But if friends continue to deliberately exclude, there comes a time when they need to move on, before this behaviour completely breaks them. If they are being subjected to ongoing exclusion, it is time to walk away.

However, they don't always choose to do this, and sometimes we can struggle with their choice of friends. As we noted earlier, during puberty the brain is growing more quickly than at any other point in childhood, however, our teens also have a newfound sense of self-consciousness. They are taking in information at an increased rate and have a stronger awareness of themselves and their peers. This makes them increasingly aware of social relationships, their own identity, and their identity within their peer group. As such, teenage brains become highly tuned in to status. For example, who is the most powerful and influential within their peers.

Likeability and Status

There are two important aspects of popularity which are necessary to distinguish between – likeability and status. Young children are drawn to likability, which can have great benefits in the school yard, and this type of popularity is important again later in life. Likeability is related to aspects such as friendliness, communication skills and social skills. In preschool and early primary school, children who can get along well with others, who include others and have a smile on their faces are well liked. Meanwhile, teens are often drawn to the other type of popularity, status. This involves power, influence, and notoriety. This has nothing to do with likeability. In fact, research shows that the most popular group, particularly with girls, are often the least liked by their peers[42]. Guided by status however, we can find our teenager desperate to develop a friendship with the Queen Bee of the class.

Keeping this in mind, it is important they learn to choose friends who add to their lives, rather than take away from them. Asking our teens what qualities of friendship are important to them can help them to focus on what they should be looking for in a friend. The friend who includes them, who considers their feelings. The friend they can laugh with, but who is also there for them when they are feeling down. Friends who allow them to truly relax and be themselves, and will accept them as they are, quirks and all.

 It Takes a Village

The world is filled with people who, no matter what you do, will point blank not like you. But it is also filled with those who will love you fiercely. They are your people. You are not for everyone and that's OK. Talk to the people who can hear you. Don't waste your precious time and gifts trying to convince them of your value, they won't ever want what you're selling. Don't convince them to walk alongside you. You'll be wasting both your time and theirs and will likely inflict unnecessary wounds, which will take precious time to heal. You are not for them and they are not for you; politely wave them on and continue along your way. Sharing your path with someone is a sacred gift; don't cheapen it by rolling yours in the wrong direction. Keep facing your true north.

[Credit: Rebecca Campbell, Light is The New Black]

For many of our children it can take time to find the ones who will become their valued friends and confidants. For some, these friends are not found in the classroom, but in activities where they share common bonds.

👍 Give it a Try!

Rather than limiting their friendship group to classmates or neighbours, joining a club or extra-curricular class can be a great way to extend their circle of friends. There are so many programmes and clubs now for various interests, from drama to chess, from coding to cookery, from photography to martial arts. Joining a group like this exposes our children to a range of new people. They often find they have more in common with children who like similar activities. Sporting clubs are also a great way to meet new people and become part of a new community.

When they are struggling with friendships, our role is to offer calm and connection. Sometimes sharing our own friendship history can help. Letting them know that not all friendships last, but that we will go on to find friends with whom we have more in common. Our role is to offer a listening ear, support when needed, and sometimes a shoulder to cry on. But we need to stand back a little and allow them to sort out any friendship difficulties themselves. We want to empower them to negotiate the complexity of teenage relationships themselves, so they grow into well-adjusted adults with strong social skills.

Communicating Versus Controlling

As they make this move away from us towards their peers, another change we can expect is many of them become allergic to control! The more we try to force their hand, the more likely they are to rebel.

During adolescence, our teens are driven by evolution to seek independence. The more we try to control them, the more we risk losing them. Instead, we can focus on providing support and guidance. Let go of our need to control, and once again focus on connection.

Instead of making them feel they are being controlled, we want them to know we respect their need for greater autonomy. We respect their need for independence, we respect their views, but we also need them to respect ours. We want them to take our requests seriously, and in order to make sure this happens, we need to make our expectations clear.

We also need them to understand that their actions have consequences. Let's not forget the skill of negotiation. They are nearing adulthood, and if we want them to understand the importance of discussion and negotiation, we need to model that behaviour. We want them to develop cognitive flexibility, allowing them to see both sides of an argument. Engaging in open discussion when agreeing boundaries is a good way of participating in healthy adult decision making.

Often when we are evaluating our conversations with our teens, we are thinking about the messages we want to get across to them, instead of thinking about what we can learn from them. We spend so much of our time in giving advice, making requests, and discussing house rules that sometimes these conversations can feel more like hostage negotiations! But remember successful negotiation in real life situations involves understanding and empathy. In order to negotiate, we need first to listen.

Trying to assert our will is destined for failure. For example, if our teenager is angry about some of our house rules, it can help to allow them the time to explain their reasons. Allow them to make their case, while acknowledging their points, before making our own case. Doing this makes them aware that we see their needs and take them seriously.

Staying calm and in control should also be our aim when communicating with our teenagers. Not always easy, I know, but it's best to avoid important conversations in the heat of the moment. Even if it means walking away and explaining you need space to think before having a discussion. Finding a time and a place when you are both calm and can speak freely is necessary. Many of us can be afraid of silences in conversation, but these can allow us time to process our thoughts. The less we talk, the more likely they will open up to us. We want them to see us as a sounding board they can go to when they need to talk through any challenges they are facing.

 It Takes a Village

Some good advice I got, particularly now I have a teen, is when you doubt yourself and your parenting, know you made the best decisions you could make at the time you made them. We do what we do from a place of love and with our best intentions. We learn more as our journey through life progresses, we need to remember we are all doing the best we can with what we know at this time.

[Credit: Lee Herlihy, via Facebook]

When our teens start to push against us, and as we know they are developmentally programmed to do this, sometimes we try to assert our control. We need to remember this push for independence is the start of their transition to adulthood, and so a very necessary developmental phase. Our natural inclination can be to try to pull them back towards us. But instead we need to maintain a balance between holding on to our connection while also accepting their need for separation. Sometimes this means trusting we have done our job and trusting they have the skills they need to navigate the adult world. Yes, they will make mistakes, but remember mistakes are part of the learning process. We want to make sure they know when this happens, if they need our support, we are there with a listening ear. Not judgement, not anger, not a lecture, but a calm listening ear available with advice if requested.

Sometimes it might seem as if our teens are deliberately being unreasonable and trying to push all our buttons. They seem to blame us for everything, and we are on the receiving end of the maelstrom of emotions whirling within them. At times like this, it can help to remember that just like our toddlers, when the world outside seems unsafe our teens need to know they are safe at home. Sometimes they need to test this out, to see if we will be there for them. Try not to take it personally, instead, take comfort in knowing you have created a safe space where they can really be themselves.

They are pushing boundaries and are worse around us because they are secure in our presence. When this is the case, all they need is our presence. Feeling safe is not about living in a perfect world. It is about living in the real world, but with the support of a loving connection.

Dealing with Strong Emotions

The teenage brain responds to emotion differently to both adults and younger children. Studies using Magnetic Resonance Imagery (MRI) have shown that our teens are very reliant on the emotional brain to process their feelings, which can make them seem overly emotional at times.

Learning from Psychology

Studies comparing adolescents to adults and younger children have shown adolescents are more likely to see emotion in the faces of others. They are also more likely to judge when others are responding negatively towards them[43]. This is important to remember when they come home to us with stories of some perceived slight from a friend or schoolmate. They may appear to be more easily irritated and moody at this age, but they are not responsible for this intense brain activity. They are more likely to rely on the emotional part of their brain and are more liable to misinterpret facial cues than we are. Their brains also have a higher chance of identifying threat in everyday situations. They experience emotional highs and lows more quickly than adults and have less control over these emotions.

Is it any wonder then that adolescent relationships are often fraught with drama? This can help to explain some of their friendship misunderstandings, difficulties with teachers, squabbles with siblings, or emotional outbursts with parents. At times these issues can seem quite irrational to us because we are responding with our fully developed prefrontal cortex, but they are experiencing the world with much more emotional intensity. From our perspective, just knowing this can change our frame of reference.

Giving your teenager time to vent can be important. If we want them to come to us and share their difficulties, it is important to allow them time to be heard. It is so tempting to cut them short if they come to you to vent, but often they just need a safe space to dump their various stresses and worries. They might not be looking to us for solutions, they simply want to be heard. You don't have to agree with what they are saying, but often they just want their feelings to be validated. No advice, no fixing, no criticism, no judgement.

Top Tip!

If they come to you to vent, simply be present, respond with a listening ear and empathy. Particularly if they are having friendship issues. Venting to us is a way of processing their feelings and taking the time to consider how to respond to challenging situations.

Remember we want them to find their own inner voice, and they can only do that if we stand back and allow them to listen to their own thoughts rather than drown them out with ours.

You may find during this push against us that tempers can flare up. The most important thing to remember when you feel there is a storm brewing, is to stay calm yourself. Pushing up against them when they are feeling strongly, seldom gets us anywhere. Remember, our teens are usually caught up in the fight or flight response when they are fighting against us. Whether they fight, showing their anger, or flight, storming off in a huff, it is the emotional response speaking. They are caught up in a storm and if we argue, or push right back at them, we have little to gain. Instead, if we can ride through that moment, until their emotions have waned, we are more likely to connect with them.

 From the Horse's Mouth

Sometimes we forget what it is like to be in their shoes. Think back to a painful moment from when you were a teenager. We all have them. A moment when someone said something about your appearance, or your family, or your ability, which cut you to the core. It may have been a deliberately inflicted wound, or even a throwaway comment. But most of us have a memory that can still bring back the humiliation we felt in that moment. Most days our teens are strong and brave, ready to take on the world. But underneath they are also fragile and vulnerable. Sometimes they cannot tell you about the pain that a comment, or a moment in time, has made them feel. Sometimes we are walking a tightrope between giving them space and letting them know we are there in the background if they need to talk.

The Quest for Perfection

We have all heard the saying, *comparison is the thief of joy*. Comparing against others with heightened expectations of perfection is another issue for teens. Many of them struggle with a constant expectation, both internally and from their peer group, of the person they should be. They should be beautiful, they should be thin, they should have a six-pack, they should be popular. The list is never ending. How hard must life be when you compare yourself to others in this way and have such high expectations of perfection in every area of your life. The fear of imperfection, combined with the high standards our teens set for themselves, may be linked to the struggle many experience in terms of body image.

 What Does the Research Say?

Dr Justin Coulson, author of *Miss Connection*[44], undertook a survey of approximately 400 girls about their concerns. More than half noted that body image was the biggest worry in their lives. Although his research is focused on girls, most parents will agree these issues apply to all of our teenagers. He refers to the three issues of *appearance, identity,* and *friends*, as the "the axis of evil," because they are so inter-related and have such a big impact on the lives of our teens.

We know appearance is very much linked to both identity and personal value and is an everyday problem for many teenagers. Coulson links this very much to an over-reliance on social media. The teenagers in his survey were very aware they were constantly being judged, and continuously looked for validation from external sources.

From the Horse's Mouth

Not surprisingly many of our teenagers are obsessed with the images they project into the world via social media. They make use of every available tool to manipulate this image, often presenting a very heavily curated version of themselves to the world. The danger is that it can be extremely hard to live up to that image. I remember a friend showing me photos of a young girl she knew on Instagram. This girl would have been late teens and her photos were usually posted half naked, at least to the eyes of the Irish Mammy ("Well, she'll catch her death of cold in that!") but she was a stunningly beautiful young girl. One day, I was introduced to this young girl in person and was shocked to see she looked nothing like the images I had been shown online. I would never have recognised her as the girl in the photos. Teens can spend hours alone in their room editing and filtering their images. However, at some point they have to leave that safe space and present their real selves to the world. I could not help but worry about the impact on this girl's emotional wellbeing. When I was a girl, we worried we could never live up to the images of the film and TV stars we admired. However, our teenagers are now faced with the reality that they cannot live up to the images of themselves which they put online.

We know our teenagers, no matter their gender, are barraged with a constant stream of pressure, both from the media and their peers, reinforcing the message that their value is based on their appearance. The pressure to look perfect is constant. The air-brushed images they see online are not realistic. Nevertheless, millions of teens desperately try to match these impossible expectations. We cannot remove the images, so instead we need to talk to them about these unrealistic representations of body image, photo-shopping etc.

But this is not enough. We need to do more. Instead of teaching our teens to tolerate difference, let's teach them to celebrate difference.

We all have different abilities, we all have strengths and weaknesses, and our own little quirks. Let's focus on diversity, inclusion, friendship, and respect. Focus on building their strengths. We can do this by being specific and praising them honestly and realistically.

👍 Give it a Try!

We sometimes believe that in order to encourage girls to see that beauty is more than skin deep, we should never comment on their looks. Of course, we should focus on recognising their talents, their intellect, their bravery, their strength. Nonetheless, we can let them know we see beauty when we look at them by reminding them they have beautiful eyes, a beautiful smile, or that they light up the room when they laugh. This is a proactive way to encourage them to see their potential in every area. The heavily curated image of beauty they see online is just one representation. Real beauty is much wider and more inclusive than that. We want them to see the beauty we see when we look at them.

Remember too that this issue is not exclusively for girls. We sometimes forget the impact on boys. Historically the quest for physical perfection was viewed as a female problem, but we now know this is a misconception. For example, we now understand that eating disorders in young men are under-diagnosed, under-recognised, and under-treated.

 What Does the Research Say?

Bodywhys, the Eating Disorders Association of Ireland[45], tell us that our boys and young men can feel pressured by body image to engage in:

- Muscularity disordered attitudes and behaviours
- A focus on muscular leanness
- Sporadic binge episodes perceived to increase muscularity
- Protein-centric binge episodes
- Excessive exercise to compensate for caloric intake
- A 'runaway diet'
- Muscle dysmorphia
- Use of steroids and growth hormones

We are very much aware of the images in the media which young girls have to deal with, however unrealistic images of muscular young men are also becoming the norm. We speak to our young girls about photo-shopping and digital enhancement of online images, but do we take the time to have the same conversations with our sons? We need to remember they are being bombarded with unrealistic images of the ideal masculine body.

The misconception that these issues are not felt by our sons can also make it harder for a boy to be open about his feelings or seek support. The stigma of attitudes towards boys and young men who present with body issues needs to be addressed by our society.

These adolescent years are formative for all our children. Instead of achieving perfection, we want our teens to focus on staying active and strong. As pressure to achieve perfection increases for all children, we play a very important role in talking about healthy body image with both our sons and daughters.

Linked to this is the importance of being a positive role model in terms of our own body image. Recent research shows for children or teens struggling with negative body image, parents have been found to be an important influence. We need to be aware of the differences between what we tell our teens and what we practice ourselves. We may well tell our children that inner beauty counts and that they do not have to change their outward appearance. However, it is still likely that if we have a negative view of ourselves, they will also be self-critical. If we are struggling to attain a positive body image is it any wonder that our teens are? However, from a positive perspective, if we can become positive role models then we can be an anecdote to media images and help our children to develop a stronger sense of themselves as being strong and healthy.

👍 Give it a Try!

Here are some ideas for conversations we might have with our tweens and teens to encourage them to have more realistic expectations about themselves:

- Talk to your teen about their strengths that have nothing to do with their appearance.
- Encourage your teen to develop these strengths, the skills and talents that make them a well-rounded person.

- Identify positive role models for your teen, ones that exemplify qualities such as compassion, empathy, and honesty.
- Avoid appearance based social comparison. Instead of commenting on a person's physical appearance, comment on their character.
- Talk to your teen about the tactics the media use to sell products, and the largely unattainable results that some advertisements suggest.
- Use a critical lens to discuss media images which present near perfect beauty, and how these images are easily manipulated.
- Talk about the harsh realities that very underweight, and highly muscular models have to ensure they maintain their body type.
- Be a positive role model in terms of your own self-acceptance, and your approach to a balanced diet and fitness.

Try to have these conversations with your teen on an ongoing basis so they become aware of the unrealistic and unattainable images they view every day and help them focus on developing a strong personal body image.

Thrill Seeking and Failure

We know our teens have less well-developed self-control than adults and are more likely to make risky decisions. This can be frightening for us as parents. It is so tempting to go back to our primitive instinct to protect them, but psychology tells us that won't help. Research has shown that teens who are less likely to make risky choices are the ones who are trusted more by their parents. We need to learn to gradually trust them with making their own decisions and slowly allow them to take control over their own lives.

Instinctively it feels much safer to take over and make decisions for them but standing back and allowing them greater autonomy is setting the scene for a more successful transition to adulthood.

We have all heard the saying that failure is a bruise, not a tattoo. Understanding this is important for children of all ages, but none more so than our tweens and teens. As we noted earlier social standing is important for this age group, and failure, particularly public failure, is often seen as devastating. As adults we know that life is a series of ups and downs, so learning they can survive and cope with the inevitable disappointments which life will bring is so important. The pain of experiencing these minor failures such as not winning the race, doing badly in a test, not being asked out by the boy you like, are what teach us that we are strong, and that we can survive failure. Yes, we might need a little time to feel that disappointment, we might need a little time to regroup our thoughts, we might need a little time to pick ourselves back up, but we can do it!

Particularly during the teenage years, these emotional bruises teach our children they can cope under difficult circumstances, that they have the internal grit to plough on and live to fight another day. Another important aspect of learning these life lessons is that these disappointments also help to build empathy. They help our children relate to their friends and peers when they are knocked down by life.

We also want them to know that despite the mistakes they might make, we love them. The most important thing is that we want them to run towards us, not away from us, if these mistakes feel overwhelming. For any parents of younger children who are thinking to themselves, "Oh, mine will never make bad decisions," please believe those of us with older children, oh yes, they will! Even the best children will sometimes make mistakes, just as we did when we were their age.

👍 Give it a Try!

Our expectations for our teens can be remarkably high, and at times unrealistic in terms of who they really are. Perhaps because these years are often leading to educational goals, we can become fixated on academics. We can get lost in the race for academic achievement and the competitive nature of the educational system. Just as when they were little ones, our teens need to grow and develop at their own individual pace, and in their own way.

Remember when they were little, and you used a ruler to measure their growth against the wall? You didn't compare them to the other children in their class. You measured them against how tall they were last year. We need to continue to do the same when they are teenagers. We should try to focus on their individual strengths and value their individuality. If we can create individual expectations for each of our children that focus on their personal strengths, dispositions, and goals, we are more likely to encourage persistence and focus.

Instead of exam grades, measure success on their hearts, their minds, and their spirits. Reward positive attitude, effort, and patience, and encourage them to find their place in the world.

The final thing we can do to support our children during this transition into adulthood is to share our own experiences. If we never share our own struggles then our children are measuring themselves against an ideal, and not a real person who has overcome difficulties themselves.

Sharing past experiences where we have struggled, failed, and recovered, or needed support to survive an event, help them to understand that none of us are perfect.

No matter how often we tell them it is OK to be imperfect and that it is OK to ask for support, if we then spend our lives seeking perfection, they will be guided by what they see, not what we say.

CONCLUSION

Flying the Nest

The teenage years are probably the ones when we feel most sympathy with our own parents and come to understand that the worry never stops. Now I finally understand why my mother said she could only sleep when all three of her children were home at night safe in their beds! It seems our role as protector never ends, but these years are the ones in which we fully learn to let go of those apron strings, while leaving our children with the knowledge that we will always be there for them.

There is no perfect way to parent our children. Every family situation is unique. We all have different strengths and abilities. Each of our children are different, and again they have different skills, personalities, and challenges. What matters most is not that we are a perfect family, but that we love them, and are there for them when they need us. We sometimes think our teens no longer need to be told that we love them, but it is so important that we continue to let them know how proud we are of them. If we want them to feel worthy, we need to remind them of the great people they are. It can be a fine balance between holding and nurturing them and letting them face life's transitions themselves.

Our job as parents is to support them to be strong enough to leave us and build a life of their own. For most of us, our goal is for our home to be the place they will always want to come back to. But what a joy it is to see our children develop into young adults.

As Kay describes below, watching your children grow into adults opens a whole new chapter to our lives. Life comes full circle, and in the future we will hopefully have the joy of watching our children become parents, as we pass on the baton of parenting to them!

 It Takes a Village

Nothing can prepare you for becoming a Grandmother! The joy and happiness grandchildren bring to your life is immeasurable. Being Grandmother to nine beautiful children is a blessing I cherish every day. It is wonderful to be able to share with them their family history and to be a part of their future. Their presence in my life makes this period of life worthwhile and gives me hope for the future.

[Credit: Kay O'Brien]

Accepting Imperfection

I started this book by saying we are all imperfect parents. We are never going to get everything right, nor should we have to. I hope that reading this book helps you to realise that perfection is not required. Instead, the most important qualities for parenting are love and connection. Recognising that imperfection is perfectly OK, helps us in our connection with our children. It takes some of the pressure off. We can forgive ourselves for past errors, and instead focus on continuing to develop as parents, along with our children's natural development.

Above all else, if our children know we love them, and we keep the lines of connection open, we will get through whatever challenges life throws at us. Parenting is a learning curve, but we are up to the task!

ENDNOTES

1. Winnicott, D. (1971). Playing and reality. New York: Basic Books.
2. Twenge, J. M. (2017). iGen: Why today's super-connected kids are growing up less rebellious, more tolerant, less happy- and completely unprepared for adulthood and what this means for the rest of us. New York, NY: Atria Books.
3. Gray P. The decline of play and the rise of psychopathology in children and adolescents. Am. J. Play. 2011;3:443–463.
4. Harlow, H. F. (1958) 'The nature of love', American Psychologist, vol. 13, pp. 673–85.
5. Bowlby J (1969) Attachment and loss, Vol. 1: Attachment. New York: Basic Books.
6. George E. Vaillant; Charles C. McArthur; and Arlie Bock (2010) Grant Study of Adult Development, 1938-2000, Harvard Dataverse,V4.
7. Godfrey M (2018) Mud Play and Mud Kitchens in Goodliff G, Canning N, Parry J and Miller L (eds) Young Children's Play and Creativity: Multiple Voices. Milton Keynes: The Open University Press
8. Covey, S. (2004). The 7 Habits of Highly Effective People. New York, N.Y.: Simon & Schuster.
9. Gino F (2018) When solving problems, think about what you could do, not what you should do. Harvard Business Review. Available at: https://hbr.org/2018/04/when-solving-problems-think-about-what-you-could-do-not-what-you-should-do
10. L.S. Blackwell, K.H. Trzesniewski, C.S. Dweck (2007) Implicit theories of intelligence predict achievement across an adolescent transition: A longitudinal study and an intervention, Child Development, 78, pp.246-263
11. Moser, J. S., Schroder, H. S., Heeter, C., Moran, T. P., & Lee, Y. H. (2011). Mind Your Errors Evidence for a Neural Mechanism Linking

Growth Mind-Set to Adaptive Posterior Adjustments. Psychological Science, 0956797611419520.

12. Sesame Street (2012) What is a Friend. Available at: https://www.you-tube.com/watch?v=iPux6QAkBdc

13. Caprara, G. V., Barbaranelli, C., Pastorelli, C., Bandura, A., & Zimbardo, P. G. (2000). Prosocial Foundations of Children's Academic Achievement. Psychological Science, 11(4), 302–306.

14. Jones D, Greenberg M, Crowley M, (2015) Early Social-Emotional Functioning and Public Health: The Relationship Between Kindergarten Social Competence and Future Wellness, American Journal of Public Health 105, no. 11: pp. 2283-2290.

15. Stade L (2017) What You Need to Know About Girls and Their Frenemies. Available at: https://lindastade.com/

16. Harvard School of Education (2014) The Children We Mean to Raise: The Real Messages Adults Are Sending About Values. The Making Caring Common Project. Available at: https://static1.square-space.com/static/5b7c56e255b02c683659fe43/t/5bae774424a694b-5feb2b05f/1538160453604/report-children-raise.pdf

17. Koster A (2018) Roots and Wings Childhood Needs a Revolution, Tipperary: Roots and Wings Publishing

18. Maccoby, E. & Martin, J. (1983). Socialization in the context of the family: Parent-child interaction. Handbook of Child Psychology Vol. 4. Socialization, Personality, and Social Development, 4, 1-101.

19. The Gottman Institute. Available at: https://www.gottman.com/blog/the-magic-relationship-ratio-according-science/

20. Tronick, E., Adamson, L.B., Als, H., & Brazelton, T.B. (1975, April). Infant emotions in normal and pertubated interactions. Paper presented at the biennial meeting of the Society for Research in Child Development, Denver, CO.

21. Leo P (2005) Connection Parenting: Parenting Through Connection Instead of Coercion, Through Love Instead of Fear. Oregon: Wyatt MacKenzie Publishing Inc.

22. Nathan Wallis, Director of X Factor Education, Australia.

23. Siegel, D. J., & Bryson, T. P. (2012). The whole-brain child: 12 revolutionary strategies to nurture your child's developing mind. Brunswick, Vic.: Scribe Publications.

24. Delahook M (2019) Beyond Behaviours: Using Brian Science and Compassion to Understand and Solve Children's Behavioural Challenges. Wisconsin: PESI Publishing

25. She can be found online at L.R. Knost – Little Hearts/Gentle Parenting Resources.

26. Cannon M, Coughlan H, Clarke M, Harley M & Kelleher I (2013) The Mental Health of Young People in Ireland: a report of the Psychiatric Epidemiology Research across the Lifespan (PERL) Group Dublin: Royal College of Surgeons in Ireland.

27. Jigsaw/UCD (2019) My World 2 Survey. Available at: http://www.myworldsurvey.ie/

28. Majdandžić, Mirjana; Lazarus, Rebecca S; Oort, Frans J; et al (2017) The Structure of Challenging Parenting Behavior and Associations With Anxiety in Dutch and Australian Children. Journal of Clinical Child & Adolescent Psychology.

29. Bolte Taylor J (2006) My Stroke of Insight: A Brain Scientist's Personal Journey. New York: Penguin Press.

30. Cohen L J (2013) The Opposite of Worry: The Playful Parenting Approach to Childhood Anxieties and Fears. New York: Ballantine Books

31. Lukianoff G and Haidt J (2018) The Coddling of the American Mind. Penguin Books.

32. Prensky M (2011) Digital Natives, Digital Immigrants. On the Horizon. 9(5) pp1-6. Available at: https://www.marcprensky.com/writing/Prensky%20-%20Digital%20Natives,%20Digital%20Immigrants%20-%20Part1.pdf.

33. Cybersafe Ireland (2019) 4th Annual Report. Available at: https://cybersafeireland.org/blog/posts/2019/september/cybersafeireland-releases-its-4th-annual-report/

34. Common Sense Media (2019) The New Normal: Parents, Teens, and Devices Around the World. Available at: https://www.commonsensemedia.org/research/The-New-Normal-Parents-Teens-and-Devices-Around-the-World

35. Steiner Adair C (2013) The Big Disconnect: Protecting Childhood and Family Relationships in the Digital Age. Harper Collins Press

36. Amy Orben, Tobias Dienlin, Andrew K. Przybylski. Proceedings of the National Academy of Sciences May 2019, 116 (21) 10226-10228; DOI: 10.1073/pnas.1902058116

37. AVG Now (2015) Kids Competing with Mobile Phones for Parents' Attention. Retrieved August 2019, Available at: https://now.avg.com/digital-diaries-kids-competing-with-mobile-phones-for-parents-attention

38. Myruski S, Gulyayeva O, Birk S, Pérez-Edgar K, Buss KA, Dennis-Tiwary TA. (2017) Digital disruption? Maternal mobile device use is related to infant socialemotional functioning. Dev Sci. 2017;e12610.

39. Pew Research Centre Survey 2020. Available at: https://www.pewsocialtrends.org/2019/01/17/generation-z-looks-a-lot-like-millennials-on-key-social-and-political-issues/

40. Erikson, E.H. (1968). Identity: Youth and Crisis. New York: Norton.

41. Heitner D (2019) Exclusion in the Instagram Age: How Can They Be Having Such a Great Time Without Me. Available at: https://www.raisingdigitalnatives.com/exclusion-in-the-instagram-age/

42. Preinstein M (2017) Popular: The Power of Likability in a Status-Obsessed World. Viking Press.

43. Siegel D J (2013) Brainstorm: The Power and Purpose of the Teenage Brain. New York: Penguin Group

44. Coulson J (2020) Miss Connection– Why Your Teenage Daughter Hates You, Expects the World and Needs to Talk. ABC Books.

45. Bodywhys, the Eating Disorders Association of Ireland (2020) Men and Eating Disorders. Available at: https://www.bodywhys.ie/understanding-eating-disorders/males-eating-disorders/

FURTHER READING LIST

Alexander J & Sandahl I (2014) *The Danish Way of Parenting: What the Happiest People in the World Know About Raising Confident, Capable Kids.* London: Tarcher Perigee

Cohen L J (2013) *The Opposite of Worry: The Playful Parenting Approach to Childhood Anxieties and Fears.* New York: Ballantine Books

Delahook M (2019) *Beyond Behaviours: Using Brain Science and Compassion to Understand and Solve Children's Behavioural Challenges.* Wisconsin: PESI Publishing.

Dweck C (2007) *Mindset: The New Psychology of Success.* USA: Ballantine Books.

Gray P (2013) *Free to learn: Why unleashing the instinct to play will make our children happier, more self-reliant, and better students for life.* Basic Books.

Golman D (1995) *Emotional Intelligence.* Bantam Books

Knost L R (2013) *The Gentle Parent: Positive Practical Effective Discipline.* Little Heart Books

Koster A (2018) *Roots and Wings: Childhood Needs a Revolution,* Tipperary: Roots and Wings Publishing

Leo P (2005) *Connection Parenting: Parenting Through Connection Instead of Coercion, Through Love Instead of Fear.* Oregon: Wyatt MacKenzie Publishing Inc.

Louv R (2005) *Last Child in the Woods: Saving our Children from Nature-Deficit Disorder* Chapel Hill, NC: Algonquin Books of Chapel Hill

O'Malley S (2017) *Bully Proof Kids*. Dublin: Gill Books

Perry B (2017) *The Boy Who Was Raised as a Dog*. New York: Basic Books.

Rotbard H (2012) *No Regrets Parenting, Turning Long Days and Short Years into Cherished Moments You're your Kids*. Miss: Andrews McMeel Publishing.

Siegel D J (2013) *Brainstorm: The Power and Purpose of the Teenage Brain*. New York: Penguin Group

Siegel D J & Bryson T P (2012) *The whole-brain child: 12 revolutionary strategies to nurture your child's developing mind*. Brunswick, Vic.: Scribe Publications

Steiner Adair C (2013) *The Big Disconnect: Protecting Childhood and Family Relationships in the Digital Age*. Harper Collins Press

Twenge J M (2017). *iGen: Why today's super-connected kids are growing up less rebellious, more tolerant, less happy-- and completely unprepared for adulthood (and what this means for the rest of us*. New York, NY: Atria Books.

Winnicott D (1971) *Playing and reality*. New York: Basic Books

Winnicott D (1988) *Babies and their Mothers* London: Free Association Books

Young K (2017*) Hey Warrior – A Book for Kids About Anxiety*. Australia: Little Steps Publishing.

ACKNOWLEDGEMENTS

This book is all about connection with our children, and I am so lucky to have worked on it with people with whom I have also felt a real connection. There are so many people I would like to thank for their support and expertise while writing his book.

Firstly, thanks to Geraldine Walsh for her editing expertise. Oh, how naïve I was when I wrote the first draft of the book. I really thought that first draft meant I was nearly there, how wrong I was! But Ger very gently guided me to consider the structure and flow of the piece, she made me think about my personal values, why I was writing the book, and what I wanted for the reader. She gave me great advice and support. If anyone reading this is considering writing a book, you need her in your life!

Thanks to Orla Kelly for her publishing expertise and professional input. I would also like to thank Alexandra Koster for her kindness and advice throughout the process. Thanks to all the wonderful authors who gave me permission to use quotations from their work in the book. I would also like to thank each of the parents and educators who let me share their 'It Takes a Village' quotes about their personal experiences. They are Sinead Connolly, Gráinne Dunne, Judy Evans, Jane Foden, Lee Herlihy, Alex Koster, Ria Megnin, Kay O'Brien, Fiona Scott and Sara White.

I also wanted to say thank you to all the wonderful parents and educators (many of whom are past students) that I connect with on social media, particularly on my Facebook page. I wanted that page to be a place where I could share things that inspire me as both an educator and a parent, things I struggle with as a parent and try to learn from, and things that just make me laugh! I have loved engaging with everyone who has commented and posted and wanted to thank you all for your support and kind words.

Thank you to Anton Savage and his team at Today FM who were brave enough to allow me onto the airwaves back in 2015. Particularly his producer Eimear Shannon who not only held my hand when I started with the show but who also encouraged me to write a parenting book. Thanks also to Orla Nolan, from Ireland AM, again back in 2015, for her gentle encouragement and faith in me. She helped me to believe that I would be up to the job of being a regular contributor to the programme, something I never thought I could do.

Thank you so much to Alison Curtis for writing the Foreword for the book. It is always an absolute pleasure to chat to her on her Today FM Weekend Breakfast show. Finally, thank you to Dr Malie Coyne, Samantha Hallows, Jen Hogan, Karen Koster, Pam Leo, Claire McKenna and Anton Savage for reading advance copies of the book for me. I really appreciate both your time and the lovely reviews.

On a personal note, I would like to mention my own mum. She is the one who instilled the value of communication within me. She gave myself, Gemma and Aideen a sense of stability, an abundance of love, and the confidence to go out into the world and find our own paths. She showed us what family means, and I am so lucky to have the support of all three of them in my life.

Thanks to all the friends who must be so sick of me talking about 'the book' at this stage. To Beany and Cathy, for your lifelong friendship and encouragement. Special mention to 'the school pals' who have been a constant support to me and are always there when I need a boost in confidence. Also, 'the Cannistown mums' for the early birds and zoom calls. Last, but definitely not least, to Isabel my walking partner, for our therapy sessions as we march around Dalgan or Tara. You have lived the writing of this book with me from day 1!

Finally, thanks to Liam, Erin, Michael and Kira. I am aware that while writing this book it has been a struggle to be present for my own family. So, once it is finally out in the world, that is my goal for myself, to spend more quality time with them. Unless I start to write the next one of course!

THE AUTHOR

Dr Mary O'Kane is a Lecturer in Psychology and Early Childhood Studies at the Open Univeristy. Her research interests include childhood transitions; self esteem and wellbeing, and the value of play. She runs a monthly Parenting Slot on Ireland AM discussing a broad range of parenting and childhood issues while also responding to viewers parenting queries. She is also a regular contributor to the Alison Curtis Show on Today FM. She gives public talks and online Webinars for parents and educators on a range of topics related to child wellbeing, parenting, and education. For more information on her work see www.drmaryokane.ie or you can follow her on social media.